RWANDA

Travel Guide 2025

Discover Gorilla Trekking, Safari Adventures, Volcanoes, and Hidden Treasures in Rwanda's Scenic Paradise

Leon V. Hull

Copyright © 2025 Leon V. Hull All rights reserved.

No part of this book may be reproduced, stored in a retrieval system, or transmitted in any form or by any means, electronic, mechanical, photocopying, recording, or otherwise, without the publisher's prior written permission, except for brief quotations used in reviews.

Disclaimer:

The information contained in this book is for general informational purposes only. The author and publisher make no representations or warranties concerning the content's accuracy, applicability, or completeness. The author and publisher disclaim any liability arising directly or indirectly from the use of this book.

TABLE OF CONTENT

INTRODUCTION 8

    Why Rwanda Should Be on Your Bucket List 9

CHAPTER 1 11

    Discover Rwanda's Allure: Culture, Wildlife, and More 11

    A Unique Blend of Nature and History 12

    Essential Travel Tips for Your First Visit 13

    Preparing for Your Rwandan Adventure: What You Need to Know 14

CHAPTER 2 17

    A Glimpse into Rwanda: History, Culture, and People 17

    Rwanda's History: From Tragedy to Triumph 17

    The Strength and Spirit of the Rwandan People 18

    Rwandan Art, Music, and Craftsmanship: A Cultural Legacy 19

    Language, Etiquette, and Local Customs 20

CHAPTER 3 22

    Planning Your Trip: Crafting the Perfect Itinerary 22

    Tailored Itineraries for First-Time Visitors 22

    Customizing Your Travel Plan for Unique Experiences 25

    Budgeting for Rwanda: How Much Will It Cost? 28

Packing Essentials: What to Bring and What to Leave Behind 31

CHAPTER 4 35

Kigali: Rwanda's Thriving Capital 35

Exploring Kigali's Past and Present 35

Must-See Attractions: From the Genocide Memorial to Local Markets 37

Dining and Shopping in Kigali: Best Spots for Foodies and Shoppers 40

Where to Stay in Kigali: Accommodation for Every Budget 46

CHAPTER 5 53

Volcanoes National Park: Gorilla Trekking and Beyond 53

Trekking with Gorillas: What to Expect 53

Exploring the Rich Wildlife of Volcanoes National Park 56

Conservation Efforts: Protecting Rwanda's Natural Heritage 59

Where to Stay: Lodging Near Volcanoes National Park 62

CHAPTER 6 68

Rwanda's Lakes: Natural Beauty and Peaceful Retreats 68

Lake Kivu: Rwanda's Stunning Lakeside Paradise 68

Hidden Gems: Lake Ruhondo and Lake Burera 71

Activities on the Water: Kayaking, Boating, and Fishing 75

Accommodations Around Rwanda's Lakes 78

CHAPTER 7 83

Nyungwe National Park: Rwanda's Tropical Paradise 83

Exploring the Biodiversity of Nyungwe Forest 83

Chimpanzee Trekking and Other Wildlife Encounters 85

Hiking Trails Nature: A Lover's Dream 88

Where to Stay: Best Lodges and Campsites in Nyungwe 91

CHAPTER 8 96

Akagera National Park: A Safari Adventure 96

The Big Five and Other Iconic Wildlife of Akagera 96

How to Make the Most of Your Safari Experience 100

Birdwatching and Boat Tours in Akagera 102

Lodging Around Akagera National Park 105

CHAPTER 9 109

Off-the-Beaten-Path Rwanda: Hidden Treasures 109

Immersing Yourself in Rwandan Culture: The Intore Dance and Local Traditions 109

Hiking Mount Karisimbi: Rwanda's Highest Peak 111

Exploring Lesser-Known Villages and Towns 114

Shopping for Local Crafts and Souvenirs 116

CHAPTER 10 121

Experiencing Rwanda: Food, Festivals, and Local Life 121

Must-Try Rwandan Dishes: A Culinary Adventure 121

Rwandan Festivals: Celebrate the Culture and Traditions 125

Traditional Crafts: A Souvenir Shopper's Guide 131

How to Connect with Locals: Tips for Meaningful Interactions 136

CHAPTER 11 139

Itinerary Planner 139

1-Week Adventure: A Comprehensive Tour of Rwanda 139

10-Day Expedition: Cultural and Wildlife Exploration 143

Nature and Wildlife Lovers: An Itinerary for the Adventurous Traveler 147

Family-Friendly Rwanda: A Tailored Travel Plan for All Ages 151

CONCLUSION 156

SCAN THIS QR CODE TO GET YOUR RWANDA MAP

After scanner the QR Code you will be linked directly to your Google Maps App, where you can now input your current location and click direction to get the exact direction from your current location to your hotel or your destination this is why you sure better scanner the QR Code for more information

INTRODUCTION

Rwanda is a country that surprises, captivates, and inspires, offering travelers a unique experience at every turn. Known as the "Land of a Thousand Hills" for its stunningly mountainous terrain, Rwanda is much more than its landscapes—it's a place steeped in history, culture, and warmth. Whether you're drawn by its wildlife, history, or the hospitality of its people, Rwanda welcomes you with open arms and invites you to connect with its story.

Rwanda's journey through time has been one of resilience and renewal. In the early 1990s, the country faced an unimaginable tragedy—the Rwandan Genocide. However, in the years since, Rwanda has rebuilt itself into a shining example of peace and progress. Today, the country is a beacon of hope, with a thriving economy, a commitment to conservation, and a strong sense of community. While history is never forgotten, it has shaped a nation that looks to the future with optimism. The culture of Rwanda is rich and varied, with influences from its 12 different ethnic groups. The majority of Rwandans practice Christianity, particularly Roman Catholicism and Protestantism, though there are also small communities of Muslims and followers of indigenous faiths. Religion plays a significant role in daily life, often guiding values such as respect for others, hard work, and family. The Rwandan people are known for their hospitality and kindness, making visitors feel like part of the community from the moment they arrive.

The currency in Rwanda is the Rwandan Franc (RWF), though US dollars are commonly accepted in larger cities. It's advisable to have some local currency on hand for smaller purchases, especially in rural areas. Rwanda's economy is steadily growing, and the country is recognized for its efforts in technology, tourism, and sustainable agriculture. The government is actively working on improving infrastructure, making travel across the country increasingly accessible.

Laws in Rwanda are strictly enforced, with a strong emphasis on safety and security. The country is known for its low crime rate and the government's dedication to maintaining peace. It's important for visitors to respect local customs, including the national ban on plastic bags, which contributes to Rwanda's clean streets and environment. Moreover, Rwanda has some of the strictest laws regarding wildlife conservation, particularly concerning the endangered mountain gorillas.

As you prepare for your journey to Rwanda, know that you're not just visiting a country; you're stepping into a story of strength, hope, and beauty. Rwanda offers an experience that will stay with you long after your departure.

Why Rwanda Should Be on Your Bucket List

Rwanda, a small but captivating country in the heart of East Africa, offers a journey unlike any other. Known for its breathtaking landscapes, it's a place where dense forests meet lush, rolling hills, and serene lakes. The land itself invites you to explore, but it's the people, culture, and wildlife that truly make Rwanda unforgettable.

First, Rwanda is home to one of the world's most famous wildlife experiences: gorilla trekking. Few adventures rival the thrill of encountering these majestic creatures in their natural habitat, a privilege that draws travelers from around the globe. Rwanda's commitment to conservation ensures that these endangered species are protected, providing an incredible opportunity for visitors to connect with nature on a profound level.

Beyond its wildlife, Rwanda offers a history of resilience. After the tragic genocide of the 1990s, Rwanda has emerged as a symbol of recovery and unity. Today, the country is one of Africa's fastest-growing economies, with an emphasis on sustainability and innovation.

Its people are warm and welcoming, eager to share their story of overcoming adversity and creating a brighter future.

Rwanda is also known for its rich cultural heritage, from traditional music and dance to the vibrant art scene. The capital, Kigali, blends modernity with history, offering a range of activities from exploring the Genocide Memorial to enjoying delicious local cuisine. Whether you're trekking through its lush national parks or engaging with its people, Rwanda offers an experience that will stay with you long after you leave.

For a vacation that combines wildlife, history, culture, and breathtaking landscapes, Rwanda is an adventure waiting to be experienced.

CHAPTER 1

Discover Rwanda's Allure: Culture, Wildlife, and More

Rwanda is a country where nature's beauty and vibrant culture converge in a truly remarkable way. Known for its spectacular landscapes, Rwanda offers much more than just picturesque views—it's a place where adventure, history, and tradition meet to create an experience that resonates long after you leave.

One of Rwanda's most captivating draws is its wildlife, particularly the endangered mountain gorillas that call the Volcanoes National Park home. Tracking these majestic creatures through the misty forests is an experience unlike any other. This country is a leader in wildlife conservation, and its efforts to protect gorillas and other species are both inspiring and essential. For those passionate about wildlife, Rwanda provides opportunities to witness some of Africa's most remarkable animals up close.

But Rwanda's appeal goes beyond its natural wonders. The country has a deeply rooted culture, one that has endured through centuries and evolved through difficult times. Rwanda's history, though painful, is a testament to resilience and hope. Today, visitors can explore this journey through sites like the Kigali Genocide Memorial, where the past is honored and remembered with dignity. The strength of the Rwandan people shines through in every encounter, whether you're exploring the local markets, enjoying traditional music, or witnessing the timeless art of the Intore dance.

Rwanda is also a place for those seeking tranquility and adventure in equal measure. From the calm shores of Lake Kivu to the dense forests of Nyungwe National Park, the country offers opportunities for hiking, birdwatching, and even zip-lining through the treetops. Whether you're looking to unwind or explore, Rwanda presents an itinerary that can suit any traveler's desires.

For those seeking a destination that combines extraordinary wildlife, rich culture, and a sense of peace, Rwanda's allure is undeniable. It's a place where every moment offers something new, and every corner invites you to connect more deeply with nature and humanity.

A Unique Blend of Nature and History

Rwanda is a place where the past and present coexist harmoniously, creating an experience that's as much about reflection as it is about adventure. The country's natural beauty is immediately striking, with its lush hills, deep valleys, and pristine lakes, all of which offer breathtaking views. Yet, it's the deep connection between Rwanda's nature and its history that truly sets it apart from other destinations.

Rwanda's landscapes have witnessed both tranquility and tragedy. The Volcanoes National Park, known for its majestic gorillas, stands as a symbol of resilience and recovery. Here, wildlife thrives amidst the beauty of the land, a stark contrast to the painful events of the past. The gorillas themselves are more than just animals to see—they are an enduring testament to Rwanda's dedication to conservation and renewal.

While the wildlife and natural wonders of Rwanda are captivating, the country's history also offers powerful lessons. The Genocide Memorial in Kigali is a place of reflection, where visitors can learn about the country's darkest chapter and witness the strength and unity of the Rwandan people. It is here that the story of Rwanda's healing unfolds—a narrative of forgiveness, reconciliation, and rebuilding.

As you explore Rwanda, you'll find that the two elements—nature and history—are intertwined in ways that enhance both. The country's commitment to preserving its natural beauty while honoring its past creates a rich and complex experience for travelers. Whether you're walking through the lush forests of Nyungwe National Park or standing in quiet contemplation at the memorials, the journey through Rwanda is one of both personal discovery and shared history.

Rwanda's blend of nature and history offers a profound experience, one that invites travelers to witness the country's remarkable transformation while connecting deeply with its soul.

Essential Travel Tips for Your First Visit

If you're planning your first trip to Rwanda, you're in for an incredible experience. From its breathtaking landscapes to its rich history, this country offers much to explore. To ensure your visit goes smoothly, here are some essential tips that will help you navigate Rwanda with ease and make the most of your time there.

1. Pack Smart Rwanda is known for its mild climate, but temperatures can vary, especially in the mountains. Pack light, breathable clothing for the day, but don't forget a jacket for the cooler evenings. If you plan to visit national parks like Volcanoes or Nyungwe, bring sturdy shoes for hiking, and always pack insect repellent, as mosquitoes are common, especially in rural areas.

2. Currency and Payments The local currency is the Rwandan Franc (RWF). While US dollars are widely accepted in larger cities, it's a good idea to carry some Rwandan francs for smaller purchases in rural areas. ATMs are available in major cities, but it's always wise to have cash on hand, particularly when exploring remote locations. Credit cards are accepted in most hotels and restaurants in Kigali.

3. Health and Safety While Rwanda is generally a safe destination, it's important to stay informed about health precautions. Make sure to take malaria prevention medication before your trip and consult with a healthcare provider for any recommended vaccines. Rwanda's medical facilities are top-notch in the city, but you should carry a basic travel health kit for emergencies.

4. Respect Local Customs Rwanda's culture is deeply rooted in respect and kindness. Always greet people with a smile, and take time to learn a few basic phrases in Kinyarwanda, such as "Muraho" (Hello) and "Murakoze" (Thank you). When visiting local villages or religious sites, be respectful and ask for permission before taking photographs.

5. Transportation Rwanda is known for its efficient and safe transportation options. In Kigali, taxis and ride-hailing apps are readily available, while buses and minibuses serve rural areas. If you're planning to visit national parks or remote locations, consider hiring a local driver or joining a guided tour to ensure a smooth journey.

With these tips in mind, you'll be well-prepared to enjoy the beauty and culture of Rwanda, making your first visit unforgettable.

Preparing for Your Rwandan Adventure: What You Need to Know

Planning a trip to Rwanda? Whether you're trekking through Volcanoes National Park to see the majestic gorillas or exploring Kigali's vibrant culture, preparation is key to making the most of your adventure. Here's what you need to know to ensure a smooth and enriching experience.
1. Travel Documents and Visa Requirements Before packing your bags, make sure you have the necessary travel documents. Most visitors will need a visa to enter Rwanda, but citizens of some countries are eligible

for a visa on arrival. It's advisable to check visa requirements well in advance. Additionally, ensure that your passport is valid for at least six months beyond your travel dates. For a hassle-free entry, apply for an East African Tourist Visa if you plan to visit neighboring countries as well.

2. Health Preparations Rwanda is a safe destination for travelers, but health precautions are essential. Malaria is present in some areas, so it's recommended to consult with your doctor about antimalarial medication before your trip. In addition, vaccinations for diseases like yellow fever, hepatitis A, and typhoid might be advised, depending on your travel itinerary. Always carry a small health kit, including any personal medications and essentials like sunscreen and insect repellent.

3. Currency and Payment Methods The Rwandan Franc (RWF) is the official currency. While larger cities like Kigali accept US dollars, it's a good idea to carry local currency for purchases in rural areas or smaller shops. ATMs are widely available in Kigali, but always have cash on hand, especially when visiting remote areas. Many hotels and restaurants accept credit cards, but it's wise to inform your bank of your travel dates to avoid any issues with card payments.

4. Packing Essentials Rwanda's climate is temperate but can be cooler in the evenings, particularly in the highlands. Pack light, breathable clothes for the day, but also bring a jacket or sweater for the cooler evenings. For those heading to national parks or hiking, good walking shoes and weather-appropriate gear are necessary. Don't forget essentials like a camera, binoculars for wildlife viewing, and a power adapter.

5. Local Customs and Etiquette Rwanda is known for its welcoming and respectful people. Learning a few words in Kinyarwanda, such as "Muraho" (hello) and "Murakoze" (thank you), will go a long way in

connecting with locals. When visiting villages or religious sites, it's important to ask for permission before taking photos. Rwandans value cleanliness, so be mindful of their efforts to keep the country beautiful, including adhering to the national ban on plastic bags.

By following these simple guidelines, you'll be ready for a memorable journey through Rwanda, where nature and history intertwine to create an experience unlike any other.

CHAPTER 2

A Glimpse into Rwanda: History, Culture, and People

Rwanda's history is a powerful story of resilience and transformation, shaped by tragedy and triumph. The strength of its people, along with their rich cultural expressions in art, music, and craftsmanship, reveals a deep connection to their roots. Understanding the local customs and etiquette will enrich your experience in this remarkable country.

Rwanda's History: From Tragedy to Triumph

Rwanda's history is a testament to the strength of its people, shaped by both immense hardship and remarkable recovery. The country's past, particularly the events of the 1994 genocide, has left a deep mark on the nation. Over the course of 100 days, approximately 800,000 people were tragically killed in one of the worst atrocities in modern history. This devastating event still echoes through the lives of many, but Rwanda has shown incredible resilience, rebuilding itself in the years since.

The journey from tragedy to triumph is not just one of survival, but also of unity and forgiveness. After the genocide, Rwanda worked to heal, with a focus on reconciliation, community building, and peace. The country has since become a model for conflict resolution, with efforts aimed at promoting harmony among its people. Today, Rwanda stands as an example of hope, where wounds have been addressed and national healing is an ongoing priority.

Part of Rwanda's recovery lies in its commitment to education, economic development, and environmental sustainability. The nation has emerged from its troubled past with a growing economy, a rising standard of living, and a clear commitment to preserving its natural environment. Rwanda's leaders have focused on creating a society built on equality, with women playing a key role in the nation's progress. In fact, Rwanda boasts one of the highest percentages of women in parliament globally, which is a significant step in empowering all of its citizens.

Rwanda's history is not simply a painful chapter but a powerful reminder of the potential for renewal. The spirit of the Rwandan people shines through in their daily lives, in the way they work together to build a peaceful, prosperous nation. Visitors to Rwanda today are greeted by a country that is stronger than ever—a place where history, culture, and hope converge, offering a truly inspiring journey for those who take the time to understand its story.

The Strength and Spirit of the Rwandan People

The strength and spirit of the Rwandan people are perhaps the most powerful aspects of the country's identity. Despite enduring one of the darkest periods in human history, Rwanda's people have demonstrated an extraordinary resilience that is truly inspiring. Their ability to rebuild and unite in the wake of the 1994 genocide speaks volumes about their determination, unity, and hope for a better future.

Rwandans take great pride in their country's transformation. Their journey from despair to progress is a testament to the power of community and collective action. Today, Rwanda stands as one of the safest countries in Africa, thanks to the dedication of its citizens and their commitment to peace. The people of Rwanda have worked tirelessly to create a society grounded in mutual respect, reconciliation, and shared values. This spirit of unity is evident in every interaction, whether it's in the bustling streets of Kigali or a quiet village in the countryside.

One of the most striking things about Rwandans is their emphasis on forgiveness and togetherness. In the years following the genocide, the country focused on healing, not through division but by fostering a culture of dialogue and understanding. The "Gacaca" courts, which allowed communities to address the past and seek justice through reconciliation, became a crucial part of Rwanda's healing process. This willingness to confront painful memories while looking toward the future has become a defining characteristic of the Rwandan spirit.

The strength of the Rwandan people is also reflected in their cultural expressions, such as music, dance, and art. These forms of expression offer a glimpse into the heart of the nation—one that refuses to be defined by its past but instead chooses to create a future of hope and growth. When visiting Rwanda, it is impossible not to feel the energy, optimism, and warmth that its people radiate, reminding us all of the power of the human spirit.

Rwandan Art, Music, and Craftsmanship: A Cultural Legacy

Rwanda's art, music, and craftsmanship reflect the heart and soul of its people. These cultural expressions not only tell the story of Rwanda's past but also speak to its future—a nation that is deeply rooted in tradition while embracing innovation and growth. Each stroke of a brush, beat of a drum, and handwoven fabric carries a message of resilience, beauty, and unity.

Art in Rwanda is a form of storytelling, where every piece has meaning, purpose, and significance. Traditional Rwandan art is often linked to daily life, nature, and spiritual beliefs. Paintings and sculptures portray local scenes, from the richness of rural life to the towering mountains that dominate the landscape. Artists skillfully use natural materials, blending them with modern techniques to create pieces that capture the essence of Rwandan culture.

Music is another central element of Rwandan culture. The country's rhythmic beats and melodies are not only for celebration but also carry deep emotional and spiritual weight. Drumming, in particular, plays an essential role in Rwandan life. It's present at ceremonies, dances, and even in rituals that have been passed down for generations. Traditional music often incorporates instruments such as the ingoma (drum), umwirongi (flute), and intore (a type of fiddle), each contributing to a sound that is distinctly Rwandan.

Rwandan craftsmanship is also an integral part of the nation's cultural identity. Handwoven baskets, often intricately designed and brightly colored, are one of the most iconic forms of craftsmanship in Rwanda. These baskets, made from natural fibers, are not only beautiful but serve practical purposes in everyday life. Similarly, Rwandan beadwork and pottery have long been a means of preserving tradition while also adapting to the needs of modern times.

Through these artistic forms, Rwanda's people have maintained a connection to their heritage while simultaneously shaping their future. Art, music, and craftsmanship are not just expressions—they are a living legacy, embodying the spirit of a country that has risen from its past to create something truly remarkable.

Language, Etiquette, and Local Customs

Understanding the language, etiquette, and customs of Rwanda will enrich your visit and help you connect more deeply with the local people. Rwanda's culture is built on respect, community, and warmth, and being mindful of these traditions will ensure you have a respectful and enjoyable experience.

Rwanda's official languages are Kinyarwanda, French, and English. Kinyarwanda, spoken by the majority of the population, is the heart of communication in the country. While many Rwandans understand and speak English, especially in urban areas, learning a few basic Kinyarwanda phrases can go a long way in showing your appreciation for local culture. Simple greetings like "Muraho" (hello) and "Amakuru?" (How are you?) will help you feel more connected to the people you meet.

When it comes to etiquette, Rwanda places a high value on respect and politeness. Greeting people with a handshake is the standard, and it's important to show respect for elders, which is an integral part of Rwandan society. If you're visiting someone's home, it's customary to remove your shoes before entering, particularly in rural areas. Additionally, it's polite to address people by their titles or honorifics, such as "Mzee" for an older man or "Mama" for a woman, showing both respect and warmth.

Rwanda is a conservative country, so it's important to dress modestly, especially in rural areas or when visiting places of worship. For example, while visiting churches or mosques, both men and women are expected to cover their shoulders and knees. Public displays of affection are not common, so it's important to be discreet when interacting with loved ones in public.

Finally, hospitality is a cornerstone of Rwandan culture. Whether you're visiting a village or a city, Rwandans take pride in welcoming guests. If offered food or drink, it's polite to accept as a gesture of respect and friendship. By being mindful of these customs, you'll gain a deeper understanding of Rwanda's vibrant culture while showing respect to the people who call this remarkable country home.

CHAPTER 3

Planning Your Trip: Crafting the Perfect Itinerary

Creating the ideal itinerary for your Rwandan adventure requires thoughtful planning and a bit of personalization. This chapter will help you craft a tailored plan that suits your interests, budget, and schedule. We'll also cover practical tips on budgeting, packing, and customizing your travel experience in Rwanda.

Tailored Itineraries for First-Time Visitors

Rwanda offers an incredible mix of experiences that cater to all types of travelers, and with some careful planning, your first visit can be everything you've dreamed of and more. Whether you're drawn to wildlife adventures, cultural immersion, or simply enjoying the natural beauty of the country, crafting a tailored itinerary ensures you get the most out of your journey. Here's a guide to a carefully planned itinerary for first-time visitors to Rwanda, including key highlights, travel tips, and an estimated budget.

Day 1-2: Arrival and Kigali Exploration
Start your adventure in Kigali, the vibrant capital city. After landing at Kigali International Airport, take time to rest and adjust to the new environment. Kigali has a lot to offer in terms of history, culture, and local experiences.

- Kigali Genocide Memorial: This poignant memorial offers visitors a deep insight into Rwanda's past, educating you about the 1994 genocide and the country's journey towards reconciliation.

- Kigali City Tour: Explore local markets, art galleries, and vibrant neighborhoods. Visit the local craft shops for beautiful handmade Rwandan goods.

Estimated Budget:
- Accommodation (mid-range): $60-$100 per night
- Meals: $10-$20 per day
- Transportation: $10 for local taxis or rideshares
- Kigali Genocide Memorial entry fee: Free, but donations are appreciated

Day 3-4: Volcanoes National Park and Gorilla Trekking
After Kigali, head to Volcanoes National Park in the northwest of Rwanda, home to the world-renowned mountain gorillas. This is a highlight of any Rwanda visit. A gorilla trekking permit is required, and it's advisable to book in advance as spaces fill up quickly.

- Gorilla Trekking: Hike through the lush forest and get the chance to see one of the last remaining populations of mountain gorillas. The trek is challenging, but the reward of spending time with these gentle giants is unparalleled.
- Optional Activities: Visit the Dian Fossey Gorilla Fund International or take a nature walk around the park.

Estimated Budget:
- Gorilla Trekking Permit: $1,500 per person
- Accommodation (luxury or lodge): $150-$300 per night
- Meals: $20-$30 per day

Day 5: Lake Kivu Relaxation
After the intensity of the gorilla trek, head to Lake Kivu, one of Africa's great lakes. It offers a peaceful retreat, ideal for unwinding and enjoying the natural beauty of Rwanda.

- Boat Tours and Beach Relaxation: Take a boat ride around the lake, or simply relax on the beach. The surrounding hills provide stunning views, and you can enjoy a leisurely lunch at one of the lakeside resorts.
- Optional Activities: Visit the nearby town of Gisenyi or go for a scenic walk in the surrounding area.

Estimated Budget:
- Accommodation: $80-$150 per night
- Meals: $15-$25 per day
- Boat Tour: $30-$50

Day 6-7: Nyungwe National Park and Chimpanzee Trekking
Finish your itinerary with a visit to Nyungwe National Park, known for its rich biodiversity and stunning scenery. Here, you can enjoy chimpanzee trekking and explore one of the oldest rainforests in Africa.

- Chimpanzee Trekking: Similar to gorilla trekking, you'll hike through dense forest to observe chimpanzees in their natural habitat.
- Canopy Walk: Experience the park from above with a thrilling canopy walk that offers breathtaking views of the forest.

Estimated Budget:
- Chimpanzee Trekking Permit: $90
- Accommodation: $100-$180 per night
- Meals: $15-$25 per day
- Canopy Walk: $50
- Overall Budget for a 7-Day Trip
- Low-End: $2,000 - $2,500
- Mid-Range: $2,500 - $3,500
- Luxury: $4,000 and above

These estimates include accommodation, meals, transportation, permits, and activities. Costs will vary depending on your travel style, the time of year, and whether you choose guided tours or self-drive options.

By planning a carefully tailored itinerary, you'll not only explore Rwanda's natural wonders but also understand the depth of its culture and history. This itinerary ensures that you leave Rwanda with unforgettable memories, having seen its wild beauty, experienced its welcoming spirit, and gained insight into its remarkable transformation.

Customizing Your Travel Plan for Unique Experiences

Rwanda offers a wide array of experiences that cater to every type of traveler. While many visitors come to see the famous mountain gorillas, the country holds a wealth of other opportunities to explore its natural beauty, culture, and history. By customizing your travel plan, you can ensure your visit is not only memorable but tailored to your interests, making it a truly unique adventure.

Start with Your Interests

When planning your trip to Rwanda, begin by thinking about what excites you most. Is it the wildlife? The history? The local culture? Rwanda has something for everyone, and by honing in on what appeals to you most, you can shape your itinerary to reflect your personal passions.

For wildlife lovers, beyond gorilla trekking, Rwanda's national parks like Nyungwe and Akagera offer unforgettable experiences with chimpanzees, the Big Five, and countless bird species. If you prefer a more relaxed trip, you can explore the serene shores of Lake Kivu or take in the beautiful landscapes with a scenic drive through Rwanda's hills.

Mix Adventure with Culture
Rwanda's cultural heritage is as rich as its wildlife, and you can add a cultural layer to your journey to make it even more meaningful. Consider visiting the Kigali Genocide Memorial, where you can reflect on the resilience and strength of the Rwandan people in the face of unimaginable hardship. Take time to visit local villages, where you can interact with artisans and learn about Rwanda's traditional crafts, such as weaving and pottery.

For a deeper cultural experience, you can join a traditional Intore dance performance, which brings Rwanda's history to life through music and movement. These cultural experiences allow you to see Rwanda through the eyes of its people, learning about the traditions that have shaped the nation.

Tailor Your Activities
The beauty of Rwanda is that many activities can be adjusted to suit your pace and interests. If you're looking for more time with nature, consider hiking one of Rwanda's scenic mountains like Karisimbi or Bisoke. For those interested in a more leisurely experience, enjoying

the vibrant markets in Kigali or a relaxing boat ride on Lake Kivu offers an opportunity to witness daily life at a slower pace.

Create a Balanced Itinerary
When customizing your itinerary, it's important to balance active pursuits with moments of rest. You may spend your mornings hiking through the forests of Volcanoes National Park, but by the afternoon, you can relax at a lodge or by the lake, soaking in Rwanda's tranquility.

Budgeting for Unique Experiences
One of the greatest advantages of customizing your travel plan is the ability to tailor your budget. The costs of activities in Rwanda can vary significantly, from the high cost of a gorilla trekking permit (which averages $1,500) to the more affordable options like visiting local museums or going on nature walks in the national parks. It's helpful to research the prices for different activities and accommodations so that you can plan according to your budget.

Estimated Budget for Customized Itinerary:
- Low-End: $1,500 - $2,000 (Budget accommodation, local transport, basic park visits)
- Mid-Range: $2,500 - $4,000 (Mid-range accommodation, gorilla trekking, cultural tours)
- Luxury: $5,000+ (Luxury lodges, private tours, multiple park visits)

By customizing your travel plan, you'll not only have the chance to explore Rwanda in a way that fits your interests but also create a deeper connection with this remarkable country. Rwanda's charm lies not only in its landscapes but in its ability to offer a truly personalized experience, allowing you to craft a trip that is as unique as you are.

Budgeting for Rwanda: How Much Will It Cost?

Rwanda is a country that offers an enriching experience, from its breathtaking landscapes and wildlife to its welcoming people. As you plan your trip, understanding the costs involved will help you manage your expectations and create a budget that suits your style of travel. While Rwanda is not the cheapest destination in Africa, it offers value for money, with a range of options that can accommodate both budget-conscious and luxury travelers. Here's a breakdown of the typical costs you can expect during your visit to Rwanda.

Accommodation Costs
Rwanda has a variety of accommodation options, from budget hostels to high-end lodges. Your choice of accommodation will significantly influence your overall budget.

Budget: Hostels and guesthouses are available in Kigali and other major towns, with prices ranging from $15 to $40 per night for a basic room. In rural areas, you may find slightly lower prices. These options typically offer basic amenities with shared or private bathrooms.

Mid-Range: For a more comfortable stay, you can expect to pay between $60 and $150 per night. Mid-range hotels often include amenities like air conditioning, Wi-Fi, and breakfast. Some of the lodges near national parks such as Volcanoes National Park or Nyungwe also fall into this range.

Luxury: If you're looking for a more luxurious experience, expect to pay anywhere from $200 to $500 per night. Luxury hotels and lodges typically offer all-inclusive packages, including meals, spa services, and guided tours. The lodges around Volcanoes National Park are particularly sought after for their views and proximity to the gorillas.

Food and Drinks
Rwanda's food scene is diverse, with plenty of options for both local and international cuisine.

Budget: Eating at local restaurants or street food stalls will cost you about $5 to $10 for a meal. Traditional Rwandan dishes like ugali (maize porridge) or ibihaza (pumpkin and beans) are commonly found in local eateries.

Mid-Range: Dining at mid-range restaurants or hotel eateries will typically cost between $10 and $20 per meal. Many places offer a mix of local dishes and international options, such as grilled meats, pasta, and salads.

Luxury: In upscale restaurants or international hotels, a meal can range from $25 to $50 or more, depending on the location and the level of service.

Transportation
Getting around Rwanda is relatively easy, but the costs vary depending on how you choose to travel.

Public Transport: The cheapest option is the public bus system, which costs between $1 and $5 for short-distance trips within cities. However, public transport may not be the most convenient for tourists, especially when traveling outside Kigali.

Private Taxi/Rideshare: For a more comfortable ride, taxis or rideshare services like Uber are available. Expect to pay around $10 to $20 for a short ride within Kigali, and longer trips outside the city may cost between $30 and $50.

Car Rental: Renting a car is a great way to explore Rwanda at your own pace. Prices for a standard car rental start at around $40 to $70 per day, excluding fuel. If you prefer a more comfortable or 4x4 vehicle, especially for visiting national parks, the price may increase to $100 or more per day.

Gorilla Trekking Permit
Gorilla trekking is one of the highlights of a visit to Rwanda, but it comes with a significant cost. A gorilla trekking permit costs $1,500 per person for a day trip in Volcanoes National Park. The permit covers park entry fees, the services of a guide, and the cost of protecting the gorillas.

Other Activities
Aside from gorilla trekking, Rwanda offers a variety of other activities that you can enjoy, including chimpanzee trekking, safari experiences in Akagera National Park, and cultural experiences such as visiting the Kigali Genocide Memorial or taking part in traditional dance performances.

Chimpanzee Trekking: The permit for chimpanzee trekking in Nyungwe National Park costs around $90.

Safari in Akagera: A full-day safari in Akagera National Park typically costs $100 to $150, including entry fees and a guided tour.

Estimated Budget for a 7-Day Trip
Budget Traveler: $1,500 - $2,000
Staying in budget accommodations, eating at local restaurants, using public transport, and participating in a few local tours or activities.

Mid-Range Traveler: $2,500 - $3,500
A combination of mid-range accommodations, eating at a mix of local and mid-range restaurants, guided tours, and some additional activities like a day safari or chimpanzee trekking.

Luxury Traveler: $4,500 - $6,000+
Staying in luxury hotels and lodges, enjoying fine dining, private tours, and exclusive experiences like gorilla trekking and full-day safaris.

Conclusion
Rwanda offers a variety of travel options to suit every budget. With thoughtful planning and a clear idea of your priorities, you can craft a trip that aligns with your financial situation while ensuring that you experience all the beauty and culture this remarkable country has to offer. Whether you're traveling on a budget or indulging in luxury, Rwanda promises an unforgettable journey.

Packing Essentials: What to Bring and What to Leave Behind

As you prepare for your journey to Rwanda, packing efficiently will make your trip much more enjoyable and stress-free. From gorilla trekking to exploring Kigali, knowing what to bring—and what to leave behind—will help you make the most of your adventure. Here's a guide to packing for Rwanda, focusing on the essentials and leaving behind unnecessary items.

Clothing Essentials
Rwanda's weather can vary depending on where you are, but it's generally mild, with cooler temperatures in the highlands and warmer conditions in the lowlands. When packing, it's best to bring versatile, lightweight clothes that can be layered for comfort.

Comfortable Walking Shoes: If you plan to trek to see the gorillas or explore national parks, durable, waterproof hiking shoes are a must. The terrain can be uneven, so a sturdy pair of shoes will ensure a safe and comfortable experience.

Light Layers: Bring lightweight clothing for the day, but also include a few warmer layers for cooler evenings and mornings, especially in the highland areas like Volcanoes National Park. A light fleece jacket or sweater will come in handy.

Rain Gear: Rwanda's rainy season lasts from March to May and again in October and November. A lightweight, waterproof jacket or poncho will be invaluable, especially when trekking in national parks. It's wise to pack a small umbrella as well.

Modest Clothing: Rwanda is a conservative country, so it's important to dress modestly, particularly in rural areas and when visiting religious sites. Long sleeves, pants, and skirts that cover the knees are appropriate.

Health and Safety Essentials
Insect Repellent: Malaria is a risk in some parts of Rwanda, so bringing insect repellent with DEET is essential, especially when trekking in forests or staying near lakes.

Sunscreen and Sunglasses: Even though Rwanda is located near the equator, it can be quite cloudy, so protect your skin and eyes from the sun with high-SPF sunscreen and quality sunglasses.

Personal Medications and First Aid Kit: If you take any regular medications, ensure you have enough for the entire trip. A basic first aid kit with band-aids, pain relievers, and antiseptic cream is also a good idea.

Technology and Documentation
Camera: Rwanda is visually stunning, and you'll want to capture every moment. A good camera, ideally with zoom capabilities, is essential for wildlife photography, especially during the gorilla trek. Don't forget extra batteries or memory cards.

Power Adapter: Rwanda uses the standard UK-style three-pin plug (type G). Make sure to bring a suitable power adapter if you plan to charge your devices. A portable power bank can be a lifesaver during long excursions.

Travel Insurance and Documents: Carry a copy of your passport, travel insurance, and other important documents. You may also need a visa to enter Rwanda, which you can obtain online for most nationalities.

Leave Behind
Excessive Luxury Items: While Rwanda is a safe country to visit, it's still best to leave behind expensive jewelry and unnecessary luxury items. It's also advisable to avoid carrying too much cash, as many places accept cards.

Plastic Bags: Rwanda has a strict ban on plastic bags. Make sure to pack reusable bags for your purchases or items you want to carry. It's a small effort that supports Rwanda's clean, green initiative.

Heavy Luggage: When trekking to see the gorillas or moving around national parks, light luggage is key. Aim for a small, durable daypack for essentials and leave bulky suitcases behind.

By packing the right essentials and leaving behind items that could weigh you down, you'll ensure that your trip to Rwanda is enjoyable and hassle-free. Rwanda's beauty, culture, and wildlife await, and being prepared will help you make the most of every moment in this remarkable country.

CHAPTER 4

Kigali: Rwanda's Thriving Capital

Kigali is a city that blends history and modernity, offering visitors a chance to explore Rwanda's past and vibrant present. From the poignant Genocide Memorial to bustling local markets, Kigali has something for every traveler. This chapter highlights top attractions, dining, shopping, and accommodation options for every budget.

Exploring Kigali's Past and Present

Kigali, Rwanda's capital, is a city where the past and present seamlessly coexist, offering a captivating blend of history and modernity. As you explore Kigali, you'll find a city that has risen from its painful history to become a symbol of growth, resilience, and hope. It's a place where the remnants of Rwanda's tragic past are honored, yet where vibrant life continues to thrive.

The most significant way to connect with Kigali's past is through the Kigali Genocide Memorial. This moving site commemorates the victims of the 1994 genocide and is a place for reflection, education, and remembrance. The memorial features exhibits detailing the events leading up to the genocide, personal stories, and photographs of those who lost their lives. It's an emotional and eye-opening experience that provides essential context for understanding Rwanda's journey of recovery. The peaceful gardens surrounding the memorial also offer a space for quiet reflection.

Moving from this somber reflection, Kigali's present is a lively contrast. Today, the city is one of the cleanest and most well-organized in Africa, filled with bustling markets, vibrant neighborhoods, and a growing arts scene. A visit to the Nyamirambo neighborhood offers a chance to see everyday life in Kigali, with its colorful shops, cafés, and welcoming locals. Here, you can enjoy a coffee at one of the many cafés or shop for unique handmade crafts and clothing at the local market.

For those looking to immerse themselves in Rwanda's contemporary culture, Kigali's art galleries and performance venues should be on your list. Galleries like Inema Arts Center showcase Rwandan art, with works that explore both the nation's past and its future. Art in Kigali reflects the spirit of hope and renewal, with bold, creative expressions that celebrate Rwanda's progress.

Kigali's thriving dining scene also represents the country's cultural evolution. From high-end restaurants to street food stalls, you'll find an array of flavors, many influenced by both local and international cuisines. Dishes like brochettes (grilled meat skewers) and Isombe (cassava leaves with peanuts) offer a taste of Rwandan tradition, while fusion restaurants provide a modern twist on African cuisine.

As you walk through Kigali, you'll experience how the city has not only recovered but has also flourished. From its historical significance to its lively present, Kigali is a city that tells a story of resilience, optimism, and transformation. Whether you're visiting the memorials, exploring vibrant neighborhoods, or enjoying a meal, Kigali invites you to understand and celebrate both its past and its ongoing journey.

Must-See Attractions: From the Genocide Memorial to Local Markets

Kigali, Rwanda's capital, offers a mix of history, culture, and modern life. While the city's serene atmosphere invites leisurely exploration, it also holds stories that demand reflection. Here are some must-see attractions that bring together the essence of Kigali—from the Genocide Memorial to vibrant local markets.

Kigali Genocide Memorial
Overview & History

The Kigali Genocide Memorial stands as a solemn reminder of Rwanda's darkest chapter—the 1994 genocide. Over 800,000 people were killed in a span of 100 days. This memorial is a place for remembrance, education, and healing. Visiting it allows travelers to reflect on Rwanda's painful history and its remarkable recovery.

Location:
KG 14 Ave, Kigali, Rwanda
GPS: 1.9490° S, 30.0637° E

Best Time to Visit:
The best time to visit is during the dry season (June to September) when the weather is pleasant for walking and outdoor reflection. However, the memorial is open year-round.

Admission:
Free, but donations are welcome to support ongoing educational efforts.

Opening Hours:
9:00 AM – 6:00 PM, seven days a week.

Getting There:

The memorial is about a 15-minute drive from the city center, and taxis or private drivers are the most convenient options. The Kigali City Bus service also passes near the area.

What to Do & See:
Explore exhibits that detail the history leading up to the genocide, listen to survivor stories, and walk through the memorial gardens. There is a special children's memorial section dedicated to the youngest victims.

Nearby Restaurants & Attractions:
- Nearby Restaurant: The Hut: A local favorite for traditional Rwandan dishes with beautiful views of the city.
- Nearby Attraction: Kigali City Tower: Offering a panoramic view of Kigali, it's a great spot for photos after visiting the memorial.

Photography Tips:
While photography is allowed, be respectful—this is a place of remembrance. A quiet, respectful approach will allow you to capture the essence of the memorial without intruding on the experience of others.

Kimironko Market
Overview & History
Kimironko Market is Kigali's largest market, known for its bustling atmosphere and vibrant displays of local produce, crafts, and textiles. It's a place to experience the pulse of local life, from traders bargaining over fresh vegetables to artisans showcasing their handmade goods.

Location:
Kimironko Rd, Kigali, Rwanda
GPS: 1.9761° S, 30.1263° E

Best Time to Visit:
Any day of the week, but the market is especially lively on Saturdays.

Admission:
Free to enter; expect to purchase goods if you plan to shop.

Opening Hours:
7:00 AM – 6:00 PM daily.

Getting There:
Kimironko is about a 20-minute drive from the city center. Taxis, motorcycle taxis, or local buses are the best ways to get there.

What to Do & See:
Wander through the colorful stalls, where you can buy everything from fruits and vegetables to clothes and art. For an authentic experience, try some local street food or buy a handwoven basket as a souvenir.

Nearby Restaurants & Attractions:
- Nearby Restaurant: Sole Luna: Known for its fresh seafood and pasta, a short drive from Kimironko.
- Nearby Attraction: Niyo Art Gallery: An inspiring art gallery that features works from Rwandan artists, located a short distance from the market.

Photography Tips:
While the market is bustling, be mindful of the local vendors—always ask before taking close-up photos of people. It's best to photograph the colorful stalls and fresh produce from a distance.

Practical Information
Laws & Rules:

- Respect the local culture and traditions, especially when visiting places like the Genocide Memorial. Modest clothing is advised when entering sacred or historical sites.
- Rwanda has a strict no-smoking policy in public spaces. Always look for designated areas.

Interesting Facts:
- Rwanda is known as the "Land of a Thousand Hills," and its lush terrain is reflected in Kigali's many hills and valleys.
- Kigali is one of the cleanest cities in Africa, thanks to its ban on plastic bags and strict waste management policies.

Dining and Shopping in Kigali: Best Spots for Foodies and Shoppers

Dining Spots for Foodies in Kigali

1. The Hut Restaurant
Description:
Located in a scenic area with panoramic views of Kigali, The Hut Restaurant is a perfect blend of traditional Rwandan flavors and contemporary dining. It is renowned for its relaxed atmosphere,

excellent service, and high-quality food, making it a favorite among both locals and visitors. The restaurant specializes in fresh, locally sourced ingredients that reflect the essence of Rwandan cuisine.

Location:
- KN 6 Ave, Kigali, Rwanda
- GPS: 1.9550° S, 30.0583° E

Contact Information:
- Phone: +250 788 304 566
- Email: thehutkigali@gmail.com
- Website: www.thehutkigali.com

What to Eat and Drink:
Must-try dishes include Ugali (maize porridge), Isombe (cassava leaves cooked with peanuts), and Brochettes (grilled meat skewers). Pair these with a refreshing Passion Fruit Juice or one of their local craft beers. For dessert, don't miss the Rwandan Banana Cake, a delicious local twist on a classic favorite.

Estimated Fees:
- Main courses: $8 - $18
- Drinks: $2 - $5
- Desserts: $4 - $6

Payment Options:
Cash (Rwandan Francs and USD), Credit cards (Visa, MasterCard)

Best Time to Visit:
Visit during lunchtime or dinner for the best experience. The evening offers a serene atmosphere with spectacular city views.

2. Sole Luna Restaurant & Lounge

Description:
If you're in the mood for a fusion of Italian and Rwandan cuisine, Sole Luna Restaurant & Lounge is a top choice. Situated in a modern and elegant setting, it offers a great selection of Italian dishes with locally sourced ingredients, making it ideal for food lovers looking for both comfort and innovation.

Location:
- KK 10 Ave, Kigali, Rwanda
- GPS: 1.9541° S, 30.0602° E

Contact Information:
- Phone: +250 788 302 016
- Website: www.soleluna.rw

What to Eat and Drink:
Try the Risotto with Mushrooms, Wood-Fired Pizza, or Seafood Pasta for a true taste of Italy with a local twist. They also serve Rwandan Wines that pair perfectly with their meals. For dessert, the Tiramisu is a crowd favorite.

Estimated Fees:
- Main courses: $10 - $20
- Drinks: $3 - $7
- Desserts: $5 - $8

Payment Options:
Cash, Credit cards (Visa, MasterCard)

Best Time to Visit:
Evenings are ideal for a more intimate dining experience, especially with the restaurant's cozy ambiance and evening lights.

Shopping Spots in Kigali: A Shopper's Guide

Kigali, Rwanda's capital, offers an array of shopping experiences, from modern malls to vibrant local markets. Whether you're looking for fashion, souvenirs, or local handicrafts, Kigali has something to offer every shopper. Here are the top three shopping destinations in the city.

1. Kigali City Tower (KCT)
Overview:
Kigali City Tower, the tallest building in Rwanda, houses a variety of shops, restaurants, and a supermarket. It's a one-stop destination for high-end shopping with international and local brands. The tower's location in the center of Kigali makes it easy to access.

Location:
KN 1 Rd, Kigali, Rwanda
GPS: 1.9576° S, 30.0630° E

How to Get There:
Located in the city center, it's a short walk or drive from major hotels like the Serena Hotel. Taxis and motorcycle taxis (motos) are common transport options.

What to Shop For:
Fashion, electronics, beauty products, and local art. You'll also find international brands and a few local boutique stores.

Currency Exchange:
Kigali City Tower has a bank and ATMs for easy access to Rwandan Francs (RWF), though credit cards are widely accepted.

Opening Hours:
9:00 AM – 9:00 PM, Monday to Saturday; Closed on Sunday.

Payment Methods:
Credit cards (Visa, MasterCard), mobile money, and cash (RWF, USD).

2. Caplaki Handicraft Village
Overview:
Caplaki is a craft village offering a variety of traditional Rwandan crafts. It's an excellent spot for souvenirs like handwoven baskets, jewelry, wooden carvings, and clothing. Visitors can interact with artisans and purchase items directly from them.

Location:
KN 6 Rd, Kigali, Rwanda
GPS: 1.9523° S, 30.0602° E

How to Get There:
Caplaki is easily reachable by taxi or moto from Kigali's city center, about 10 minutes by car.

What to Shop For:
Handmade crafts, wooden sculptures, woven baskets, traditional fabrics, and jewelry.

Bargaining:
Bargaining is common here, so don't be afraid to negotiate prices. Start by offering 50-60% of the asking price and meet in the middle.
Opening Hours:

9:00 AM – 6:00 PM, Monday to Saturday.

Payment Methods:
Cash (RWF, USD), mobile money.

3. Union Trade Center (UTC)
Overview:
A shopping mall with a mix of retail shops, restaurants, and supermarkets, UTC is one of Kigali's well-known commercial hubs. It's ideal for purchasing clothing, electronics, and everyday essentials.

Location:
KN 2 Ave, Kigali, Rwanda
GPS: 1.9501° S, 30.0573° E

How to Get There:
UTC is located within the central business district, easily accessible by taxi, moto, or on foot from nearby hotels.

What to Shop For:
Clothing, accessories, electronics, cosmetics, and groceries. It's a great place for convenience shopping.

Currency Exchange:
ATMs are available inside the mall for easy cash withdrawal in local currency.

Opening Hours:
9:00 AM – 7:00 PM, Monday to Saturday; Closed on Sunday.

Payment Methods:
Cash (RWF, USD), credit cards, and mobile money.
Practical Information

Safety:
Kigali is known for its safety, but always stay aware of your surroundings. Keep your valuables secure and avoid carrying large amounts of cash when possible.

Haggling Etiquette:
While haggling is common in local markets, it's important to maintain respect and politeness during negotiations. Many shopkeepers expect a bit of back-and-forth, but try not to be aggressive.

Language:
While Kinyarwanda is the most spoken language, English and French are widely understood, especially in more commercial areas like malls and markets. It's always appreciated if you learn a few basic Kinyarwanda phrases to engage with locals.

Where to Stay in Kigali: Accommodation for Every Budget

Kigali, Rwanda's capital, offers a variety of accommodation options that cater to different tastes and budgets. Whether you're looking for luxury, comfort, or a more budget-friendly option, Kigali has places to suit every type of traveler. Here are the top five places to stay in Kigali, each offering a unique experience.

1. Kigali Serena Hotel
Description:
Kigali Serena Hotel is one of the most renowned luxury hotels in Rwanda, combining exceptional service, modern amenities, and traditional African design. Perfect for both business and leisure travelers, it offers a tranquil escape in the heart of Kigali.
Official Website: www.serenahotels.com

Property Amenities:
- Outdoor pool
- Spa and wellness center
- Fitness center
- Free Wi-Fi
- Business center and conference facilities
- On-site restaurant with international cuisine
- Airport shuttle service

Room Features & Types:
Rooms are spacious and stylishly furnished, with air conditioning, a flat-screen TV, mini bar, and a work desk. Options include deluxe rooms, executive rooms, and suites, all designed to provide maximum comfort.

Advantages:
- Central location, making it easy to explore Kigali
- Excellent service and amenities
- Great for business and leisure travelers
- Secure and upscale environment

Disadvantages:
- Higher price point compared to other hotels
- Can be busy with corporate events and conferences
- Location:
- KN 3 Avenue, Kigali, Rwanda
- GPS: 1.9571° S, 30.0975° E

How to Get There:
It's a 20-minute drive from Kigali International Airport. Taxis and private transfers are easily accessible.

2. Hotel Des Mille Collines

Description:
Made famous as the backdrop of the movie Hotel Rwanda, Hotel Des Mille Collines combines history with luxury. Offering an elegant stay in Kigali, it's ideal for those seeking comfort with a cultural experience.

Official Website: www.millecollines.kigalihotels.com

Property Amenities:
- Outdoor pool and garden
- Fitness center
- Spa services
- Free Wi-Fi
- On-site restaurants and bar
- Meeting and event spaces

Room Features & Types:
Rooms are spacious and include classic rooms, deluxe rooms, and suites. Features include air conditioning, mini bar, satellite TV, and a safe. Many rooms offer panoramic views of the city.

Advantages:
- Rich historical significance
- Great location near Kigali's central business area
- Excellent for both business and leisure stays

Disadvantages:

- Can be pricey for some budgets
- Older decor may not appeal to those seeking more modern designs

Location:
- Rue du Lac, Kigali, Rwanda
- GPS: 1.9527° S, 30.1002° E

How to Get There:
Located just a 15-minute drive from the airport, easily accessible by taxi or rideshare.

3. Radisson Blu Hotel & Convention Centre Kigali

Description:
Radisson Blu Hotel offers a contemporary stay with all the amenities you expect from a global hotel chain. This is a perfect option for travelers seeking modern design, excellent service, and easy access to Kigali's business district.

Official Website: www.radissonhotels.com

Property Amenities:
- Outdoor pool
- Full-service spa
- Fitness center
- Multiple dining options
- Conference facilities
- Airport shuttle service

Room Features & Types:
The hotel offers standard rooms, business class rooms, and suites, all equipped with modern furnishings, flat-screen TVs, minibars, and free Wi-Fi.

Advantages:
- Modern and stylish design
- Excellent service and amenities
- Perfect for business travelers

Disadvantages:
- Slightly expensive
- Large and corporate-focused, may lack local character for some visitors

Location:
- KG 2 Roundabout, Kigali, Rwanda
- GPS: 1.9549° S, 30.1178° E

How to Get There:
Located 30 minutes from the airport, easily accessible by taxi or private transfer.

4. The Manor Hotel

Description:
For those looking for a more boutique experience, The Manor Hotel offers a blend of comfort, affordability, and a personal touch. Located just outside the city center, it provides a quiet escape while still being close to Kigali's major attractions.

Official Website: www.manorkigali.com

Property Amenities:
- Outdoor pool
- Free Wi-Fi
- On-site restaurant and bar
- Garden and terrace area
- Conference facilities

Room Features & Types:
The Manor Hotel offers simple, clean rooms with modern amenities. Rooms are equipped with air conditioning, flat-screen TVs, minibars, and work desks. Room types include standard and deluxe options.

Advantages:
- Affordable compared to larger hotels
- Quiet, residential area
- Personalized service

Disadvantages:
- Located a bit farther from Kigali's city center
- Fewer amenities compared to luxury hotels

Location:
- KG 9 Ave, Kigali, Rwanda
- GPS: 1.9265° S, 30.0958° E

How to Get There:
A 20-minute drive from the airport, reachable by taxi or rideshare.

5. Mantis Kigali Sky Hotel

Description:
The Mantis Kigali Sky Hotel is an upscale option offering breathtaking views of the city. Known for its modern design and excellent service, it's ideal for those looking for a luxurious stay with panoramic views.
Official Website: www.mantiscollection.com

Property Amenities:
- Rooftop restaurant and bar with city views
- Fitness center
- Free Wi-Fi
- Business center
- Outdoor pool

Room Features & Types:
Rooms feature contemporary furnishings with city views. Options include standard rooms, deluxe rooms, and suites. All rooms come with flat-screen TVs, minibars, and safes.

Advantages:
- Excellent views of Kigali
- Modern, stylish interiors
- Convenient for both business and leisure travelers

Disadvantages:
- High price point
- Limited on-site dining options

Location:
- KN 2 Ave, Kigali, Rwanda
- GPS: 1.9493° S, 30.0616° E

How to Get There:
Located 25 minutes from Kigali International Airport, accessible by taxi or private transport.

CHAPTER 5

Volcanoes National Park: Gorilla Trekking and Beyond

Volcanoes National Park offers an unforgettable adventure with its famous gorilla trekking experiences. This chapter explores what to expect during your trek, the park's incredible wildlife, and Rwanda's efforts in conservation. Learn about the best lodging options near the park for an unforgettable stay amidst nature's wonders.

Trekking with Gorillas: What to Expect

Trekking with gorillas in Rwanda's Volcanoes National Park is a once-in-a-lifetime adventure that draws travelers from all over the world. The park, located in the northwest of the country, offers one of the best opportunities to observe endangered mountain gorillas in their natural habitat. Here's everything you need to know about this extraordinary experience.

Overview and History

Volcanoes National Park, established in 1925, is famous for its gorilla population and played a pivotal role in the conservation of these magnificent creatures. Over the years, the park has been central to Rwanda's efforts to protect mountain gorillas, a species that was once on the brink of extinction. Today, it is one of the best places in the world to see gorillas up close, thanks to years of dedicated conservation work by the Rwandan government and international wildlife organizations.

Why Visit Volcanoes National Park

The park is not just home to gorillas; it is a sanctuary for rich biodiversity, including golden monkeys and various bird species. The experience of trekking through dense bamboo forests, hearing the sounds of wildlife around you, and coming face to face with a family of gorillas is both humbling and awe-inspiring. It's a rare opportunity to witness these creatures in their natural environment and to learn about the crucial conservation work that supports them.

Location
Address:
Volcanoes National Park, Musanze, Rwanda
GPS: 1.4939° S, 29.8832° E

How to Get There:
The park is located about a 2.5-hour drive from Kigali, the capital city. It's best to hire a local driver or join a tour group, as the roads can be winding and hilly. Kigali's public transport system can also connect you to the park via buses or taxis.

Best Time to Visit
The best time to trek with the gorillas is during the dry seasons, from June to September and December to February. This is when the weather is more predictable, and the trails are less muddy, making trekking easier.

Admission Tickets and Costs
A gorilla trekking permit in Volcanoes National Park costs $1,500 per person. This fee includes park entry, the services of a guide, and the support of rangers and trackers. It's highly recommended to book your permits in advance, as spots fill up quickly, especially during peak season.

Opening Hours

The park is open daily, and gorilla trekking tours usually start early in the morning, around 7:00 AM, to make the most of the day.

What to Do and See
Aside from gorilla trekking, Volcanoes National Park offers a variety of activities:

- Golden Monkey Trekking: This is another popular activity in the park. Golden monkeys are a fun species to observe, known for their playful behavior.
- Hiking Mount Karisimbi: For adventurous trekkers, hiking Mount Karisimbi, Rwanda's highest peak, offers spectacular views of the park and surrounding areas.
- Visiting Dian Fossey's Tomb: Dian Fossey was a renowned conservationist who dedicated her life to studying and protecting mountain gorillas. Her tomb is located in the park, and a hike to it provides a chance to learn more about her legacy.

Nearby Restaurants & Attractions
- Nearby Restaurant: Five Volcanoes Boutique Hotel offers a lovely place for a meal after your trek, with views of the surrounding volcanoes.
- Nearby Attraction: Musanze Caves: Just a short drive from the park, these caves are a great spot for history and nature lovers.

Photography Tips
While photography is encouraged, ensure you follow the park's rules. Keep a respectful distance from the gorillas and avoid using flash, as it can disturb them. Use a telephoto lens for close-up shots, as getting too close may interfere with the animals' natural behavior.
Laws and Rules

- Permits: You must have a valid permit to trek with the gorillas. These can be obtained through Rwanda Development Board (RDB).
- Safety: Maintain a safe distance of at least 7 meters from the gorillas.
- Environmental Responsibility: Respect the environment by not leaving trash behind and staying on designated trails.

Interesting Facts
- Gorilla Families: Volcanoes National Park is home to around 10 habituated gorilla families that are regularly visited by trekkers.
- Conservation Success: Thanks to conservation efforts, the mountain gorilla population has increased over the past few decades, offering hope for other endangered species.

Volcanoes National Park is a once-in-a-lifetime experience for nature lovers and wildlife enthusiasts. Whether you're trekking with gorillas or exploring the rich biodiversity of the park, it's an adventure you won't soon forget.

Exploring the Rich Wildlife of Volcanoes National Park

Volcanoes National Park, located in the northwest of Rwanda, is one of Africa's most spectacular wildlife destinations. The park is famous for its mountain gorillas, but it is also home to a rich variety of other animals, making it a must-visit for nature lovers and wildlife enthusiasts.

Overview

The park spans over 160 square kilometers and is part of the Virunga Conservation Area, which also includes parts of Uganda and the Democratic Republic of Congo. It's set against the backdrop of five volcanoes, which not only create an awe-inspiring landscape but also provide the habitat for some of Africa's most iconic wildlife. Volcanoes National Park is most well-known for its gorilla population, but it also houses other animals such as golden monkeys, forest elephants, and an array of bird species.

Gorillas and Golden Monkeys
While trekking with the gorillas is the main attraction, the park also offers a chance to see golden monkeys. These bright, lively creatures inhabit the bamboo forests of the park and are frequently seen during nature walks. A golden monkey trek provides a chance to interact with a species that is rare to encounter elsewhere.

The mountain gorillas, however, are the stars of the show. The park is home to roughly half of the world's remaining mountain gorillas. Trekking through the dense forest to see them up close is an unforgettable experience. Observing these gentle giants in their natural habitat is both humbling and awe-inspiring. The gorillas' social behavior, such as grooming, playing, and interacting with their young, offers visitors a rare glimpse into their world.

Other Wildlife in the Park
Besides gorillas and golden monkeys, Volcanoes National Park is home to a variety of other wildlife, including the elusive forest elephants. These smaller cousins of the savannah elephants are harder to spot but are a significant part of the park's ecosystem. The park also offers a wealth of birdlife, making it a fantastic destination for bird watchers. Species like the Rwenzori turaco and the white-necked raven are often spotted among the park's dense vegetation.
What to Do and See

- Gorilla Trekking: The primary attraction, where you can hike through the forest and meet a family of gorillas.
- Golden Monkey Trekking: A fun alternative for those who want to see a different side of the park's wildlife.
- Nature Walks: Explore the bamboo forests, home to many species, including the rare golden monkey.
- Bird Watching: With over 200 bird species in the park, it's an excellent spot for birding.

Best Time to Visit

The best time to visit Volcanoes National Park is during the dry season, from June to September and December to February. During these months, the trails are easier to navigate, and the chances of seeing wildlife are higher. The wet season (March to May) can make trekking more challenging, but it's also the least crowded time of year.

Practical Information
- Admission Fees: Gorilla trekking permits are priced at $1,500 per person, while golden monkey trekking permits cost about $100.
- How to Get There: Volcanoes National Park is about a 2.5-hour drive from Kigali. Private transportation or guided tours are the most convenient options.
- What to Bring: Good hiking boots, a waterproof jacket, a walking stick (provided by the park), and a camera with a zoom lens for wildlife photography.

Nearby Restaurants and Attractions
- Nearby Restaurant: Five Volcanoes Boutique Hotel offers both local and international dishes and is a great place to relax after a day of trekking.

- Nearby Attraction: Dian Fossey's Tomb: A short hike takes you to the tomb of the famous gorilla conservationist, Dian Fossey, providing insight into her efforts to protect these magnificent creatures.

Photography Tips
While photographing wildlife, be respectful. Avoid using flash, as it can disturb the animals. A long lens is ideal for capturing the gorillas and other wildlife without intruding on their space.

Interesting Facts
Volcanoes National Park was the site of Dian Fossey's groundbreaking research on mountain gorillas, which played a significant role in their conservation.

The park is one of the most successful wildlife conservation areas in Africa, with the mountain gorilla population steadily increasing.
In Volcanoes National Park, visitors not only have the chance to witness one of the world's most remarkable conservation successes but also experience a profound connection to the natural world. Whether you're trekking with gorillas or observing other wildlife, the park offers an unforgettable journey.

Conservation Efforts: Protecting Rwanda's Natural Heritage

Rwanda is renowned for its steadfast commitment to conservation, and Volcanoes National Park is a shining example of these efforts. This lush, biodiverse park, which covers 160 square kilometers, is home to the endangered mountain gorillas and a variety of other species. Over the years, Rwanda has become a leader in wildlife conservation, and the park plays a key role in this success story.

The Gorilla Conservation Program
The mountain gorillas in Volcanoes National Park are at the center of Rwanda's conservation initiatives. In the early 1980s, the gorilla population was rapidly declining due to poaching, habitat destruction, and diseases. In response, conservation efforts were ramped up. With support from international organizations, the government, and local communities, the population of mountain gorillas in Rwanda has steadily increased. Today, Volcanoes National Park is home to nearly half of the world's remaining mountain gorillas.

Tourism has played an essential role in these efforts. Gorilla trekking has become a major eco-tourism attraction, generating revenue that is reinvested in conservation activities. By offering gorilla trekking permits, Rwanda has created a sustainable income stream that supports wildlife protection and helps fund community programs.

Community Involvement
One of the most powerful aspects of Rwanda's conservation strategy is the involvement of local communities. Conservationists understand that protecting wildlife and natural resources requires the support of those who live in and around the park. To ensure the sustainability of the park's ecosystem, locals have been trained as park rangers, guides, and eco-tourism operators.

Additionally, Rwanda's government has encouraged community-based tourism, which directly benefits local populations by providing jobs and economic opportunities. Villages near Volcanoes National Park have developed projects to educate locals on the importance of conservation, reducing human-wildlife conflict and fostering a culture of respect for nature.

Protection of Habitats
Rwanda's conservation efforts go beyond just the gorillas. The entire ecosystem of Volcanoes National Park is carefully managed to protect its wildlife. The park's forests, grasslands, and volcanic mountains are home to many rare species, including golden monkeys, forest elephants, and a wide variety of birds.

To preserve these habitats, ongoing anti-poaching measures are enforced. Regular patrols, surveillance technology, and strict regulations ensure that the park remains a safe haven for its wildlife. Invasive plant species are also controlled, allowing native vegetation to thrive and support the overall health of the ecosystem.

Sustainable Tourism Practices
As one of Rwanda's most visited parks, Volcanoes National Park also emphasizes sustainable tourism practices. Visitors to the park are encouraged to respect wildlife, stay on designated trails, and minimize their impact on the environment. The park has a strict policy on limiting the number of visitors allowed for gorilla trekking each day to ensure that the gorillas are not disturbed and that their natural behaviors are preserved.

What's Next for Volcanoes National Park?
Rwanda's commitment to conservation continues to evolve, with plans to expand the park's boundaries and protect more of the surrounding ecosystem. The government is also working on reintroducing species that were once native to the region but have since disappeared, such as the black rhino. These efforts show Rwanda's dedication to preserving its natural heritage for future generations.

Volcanoes National Park is not just a place of natural beauty; it is a symbol of Rwanda's dedication to wildlife protection and environmental sustainability. By visiting the park, you are contributing to these efforts and supporting the ongoing protection of the mountain gorillas and their habitat.

Where to Stay: Lodging Near Volcanoes National Park

Volcanoes National Park is a top destination in Rwanda for trekking with gorillas and experiencing breathtaking natural beauty. After a day of trekking, you'll want to rest in comfort. Here are the best lodging options near the park, each offering unique features and experiences for visitors.

1. Bisate Lodge
Description:
Bisate Lodge is a luxurious eco-lodge that provides an exclusive and intimate experience near Volcanoes National Park. Designed to blend with the landscape, the lodge offers stunning views of the park and surrounding volcanoes, making it an ideal spot for travelers seeking comfort and a closer connection to nature.

Official Website: www.bisatelodge.com

Property Amenities:
- Heated plunge pools
- Restaurant serving local and international cuisine
- Spa services
- Guided nature walks
- Free Wi-Fi
- Airport shuttle

Room Features & Types:
The lodge offers six luxurious forest villas, each with panoramic views, a comfortable bed, a fireplace, a private deck, and an en-suite bathroom. The villas are designed with eco-friendly materials and feature Rwandan-inspired décor.

Advantages:
- Stunning location with views of the Volcanoes
- High level of luxury and privacy
- Excellent service with personalized experiences
- Eco-friendly design and operations

Disadvantages:
- Expensive compared to other lodges
- Limited number of rooms, making it difficult to book during peak season

Location:
- Bisate Lodge, Volcanoes National Park, Rwanda
- GPS: 1.4858° S, 29.8841° E

How to Get There:
A 2.5-hour drive from Kigali. The lodge offers airport transfer services and can arrange transportation upon request.

2. Sabyinyo Silverback Lodge
Description:
Sabyinyo Silverback Lodge is another top-tier lodge near Volcanoes National Park. It's known for its breathtaking views, spacious rooms, and commitment to sustainability. The lodge provides a comfortable and relaxing base for gorilla trekking and offers a range of activities that make the most of its location.

Official Website: www.sabyinyosilverbacklodge.com

Property Amenities:
- On-site restaurant and bar
- Spa and wellness center
- Free Wi-Fi
- Guided tours and treks
- Gift shop
- Airport shuttle

Room Features & Types:
The lodge has spacious cottages with large windows that provide expansive views of the volcanoes and the surrounding forest. Each cottage has a fireplace, private terrace, en-suite bathroom, and sitting area. There are also family cottages available.

Advantages:
- Stunning views of Volcanoes National Park
- Spacious, comfortable rooms
- High-quality service and excellent dining
- Close proximity to the park entrance

Disadvantages:
- Prices can be steep
- Not as private as smaller, more exclusive lodges

Location:
- Sabyinyo Silverback Lodge, Kinigi, Rwanda
- GPS: 1.4961° S, 29.8761° E

How to Get There:
Located just a short drive from the park entrance, approximately 2.5 hours from Kigali.

3. Mountain Gorilla View Lodge

Description:
Mountain Gorilla View Lodge is a great option for those looking for comfort without the hefty price tag. Located near Volcanoes National Park, it offers stunning views of the volcanoes and easy access to trekking activities.

Official Website: www.mountain-gorilla-view-lodge.com

Property Amenities:
Restaurant and bar
- Laundry services
- Gift shop
- Free Wi-Fi
- Shuttle services
- Conference facilities

Room Features & Types:
The lodge features comfortable rooms and cottages, each with a private terrace, en-suite bathroom, and simple, traditional décor. The cottages offer a warm and inviting atmosphere, making it an excellent base for gorilla trekking.

Advantages:
- Budget-friendly compared to other lodges in the area
- Spacious rooms with beautiful views
- Proximity to Volcanoes National Park
- Friendly and accommodating staff

Disadvantages:
- Simpler amenities and less luxurious than high-end options
- The décor is a bit basic

Location:
- Mountain Gorilla View Lodge, Kinigi, Rwanda
- GPS: 1.4976° S, 29.8765° E

How to Get There:
A short drive from the park entrance. Approximately 2.5 hours from Kigali by car.

4. Virunga Lodge

Description:
Virunga Lodge is one of the most popular and scenic lodges near Volcanoes National Park. The lodge offers unparalleled views of the Virunga Volcanoes and Lake Ruhondo. It's ideal for those seeking a more luxurious stay with exceptional service.

Official Website: www.virungalodge.com

Property Amenities:
Private dining experience
- Lounge and bar area
- Spa treatments
- Free Wi-Fi
- Guided tours and treks
- Airport shuttle

Room Features & Types:
Virunga Lodge has ten spacious rooms, each with a private terrace offering panoramic views. The rooms are designed with luxury and

comfort in mind, featuring en-suite bathrooms, large beds, and unique wooden furnishings.

Advantages:
- Exceptional views of the volcanoes and Lake Ruhondo
- Luxurious rooms with great comfort
- Personalized service
- Close to trekking sites

Disadvantages:
- High cost for most travelers
- Limited number of rooms, especially during peak seasons

Location:
- Virunga Lodge, Kinigi, Rwanda
- GPS: 1.5103° S, 29.8862° E

How to Get There:
A 2.5-hour drive from Kigali. Transfers to and from the park are available upon request.

Whether you're looking for luxury or a more budget-friendly option, these lodges near Volcanoes National Park offer great accommodation for your stay. Each lodge offers a unique experience and serves as the perfect base for your gorilla trekking adventure.

CHAPTER 6

Rwanda's Lakes: Natural Beauty and Peaceful Retreats

Rwanda's lakes offer serene retreats surrounded by breathtaking landscapes. From the picturesque shores of Lake Kivu to the tranquil beauty of Lake Ruhondo and Lake Burera, these natural wonders provide the perfect escape. Explore peaceful activities like kayaking, boating, and fishing, and enjoy nearby accommodations for a restful stay.

Lake Kivu: Rwanda's Stunning Lakeside Paradise

Lake Kivu, one of the largest lakes in East Africa, is an idyllic destination for visitors looking to combine natural beauty with outdoor adventure. Located along Rwanda's western border, this freshwater lake is framed by lush hills and offers a wide variety of activities, from kayaking to hiking, making it a prime spot for nature lovers and thrill-seekers alike.

Best Places for Outdoor Adventures
Lake Kivu is an adventure haven. Whether you're exploring the waters or enjoying the surrounding hills, the area offers countless opportunities:

- Kayaking & Canoeing: Paddle along the shores or venture out to small islands scattered across the lake. The calm waters make it perfect for beginners, while the stunning scenery enhances the experience.

- Hiking: Trek through the lush hills that surround the lake. The Rwankuba Peninsula and the Nyundo region are especially popular for hiking with scenic views of the lake below.
- Swimming & Boating: Many visitors enjoy swimming in the lake's clear, refreshing waters. Local boats also offer tours of the lake's remote islands.
- Fishing: Lake Kivu's abundance of fish species makes it a great spot for both recreational and local fishing.

Brief Overview

Lake Kivu spans 2,700 square kilometers and is one of the most scenic locations in Rwanda. It lies between the Democratic Republic of Congo and Rwanda, offering views of nearby volcanic mountains. The lake's tranquil waters and surrounding hills make it a peaceful retreat and an area with rich biodiversity.

Costs
- Kayaking: Typically, rental fees range from $15 to $30 per hour, depending on the type of kayak and the operator.
- Boating: Boat tours cost around $25 to $50, depending on the length of the tour and whether it includes visits to nearby islands.
- Fishing: A day's rental for a boat and fishing gear can cost approximately $40.

Seasonal Considerations
- The best time to visit is during the dry season, from May to September, when the weather is ideal for outdoor activities.
- The rainy season (October to April) brings lush green landscapes but can also make some activities more challenging due to muddy trails.

Safety Tips and Guidelines
- Always wear a life jacket when kayaking or boating.
- Follow local safety regulations for water activities, especially during windy conditions.
- Stick to established trails when hiking, as the terrain can be steep and slippery.

Permits and Regulations
- Most activities on the lake require minimal permits, such as for fishing or boating. It's best to check with local authorities or tour operators for specific requirements.
- Respect the local environment and wildlife. Do not disturb local flora or fauna and avoid littering.

Difficulty Level and Duration
Kayaking is beginner-friendly, while hiking trails around Lake Kivu range from easy to moderate in difficulty. Some hiking routes can take a few hours to a full day, depending on the destination.

Packing List
- Comfortable hiking shoes
- Light, breathable clothing for water activities
- Sun protection (hat, sunglasses, sunscreen)
- Water-resistant bags or dry bags for valuables
- Camera or smartphone for photos
- Insect repellent

Environmental Awareness
Lake Kivu and its surroundings are sensitive ecosystems. Be mindful of your environmental impact by adhering to eco-friendly travel practices such as reducing plastic use and disposing of waste responsibly.

Emergency Contacts
Rwanda Tourism Board: +250 252 573 413
Local Health Facilities: Nyundo Hospital: +250 788 300 248

Recommended Tour Operators and Guides
- Kivu Boat Tours
  Website: www.kivoboattours.com
  Offers boat rides and water-based activities on Lake Kivu.

- Kivu Hiking Adventures
  Website: www.kivuhiking.com
  Specializes in guided hikes around the Lake Kivu region.

Lake Kivu provides a perfect combination of relaxation and adventure, making it an ideal place to explore Rwanda's natural beauty while engaging in thrilling outdoor activities. Whether you're kayaking, hiking, or simply enjoying the view, it's a spot that will leave a lasting impression.

Hidden Gems: Lake Ruhondo and Lake Burera

Rwanda is known for its remarkable landscapes, and Lake Ruhondo and Lake Burera, located in the northern part of the country, stand as hidden gems that offer both tranquility and beauty, away from the more popular tourist spots.

Lake Ruhondo: A Peaceful Retreat
Overview & History
Lake Ruhondo, with its calm waters surrounded by rolling hills, is an untouched paradise. The lake is part of Rwanda's Virunga Mountain Range, adding a mystical quality to its landscape. Though less visited,

the lake holds deep cultural significance for local communities and offers a serene getaway from the busier areas of Rwanda.

Location & GPS
Located in the northern province, near the town of Musanze.
GPS: 1.5617° S, 29.5820° E

Why Visit
For those looking for quiet contemplation or a picturesque backdrop for outdoor activities, Lake Ruhondo is perfect. The lush surroundings offer ample opportunities for hiking, fishing, and boat rides, making it an ideal destination for nature lovers.

Best Time to Visit
The dry season from May to September is the best time to visit, as the weather is more favorable for outdoor activities.

Admission Tickets
Access to the lake is free, but if you plan to take part in organized activities like boat rides or fishing, prices vary.

How to Get There
Lake Ruhondo is about a 45-minute drive from Musanze, the closest town. It can be accessed by private transport or guided tours.

What to Do & See
- Boat Tours: Take a boat ride across the lake to fully appreciate the stunning views.
- Fishing: Try your hand at local fishing.
- Hiking: Explore the surrounding hills for panoramic views of the lake and the Virunga Mountains.

Nearby Restaurants & Attractions
- Restaurant: Five Volcanoes Boutique Hotel, offers local and international cuisine.
- Attraction: Volcanoes National Park, a short drive away, for gorilla trekking.

Lake Burera: A Hidden Paradise

Overview & History
Lake Burera, located near Lake Ruhondo, is another hidden treasure, surrounded by steep hills and thick vegetation. The area has a rich history and is a peaceful escape into Rwanda's natural beauty. Local communities around the lake rely on it for fishing and agriculture.

Location & GPS
Just a few kilometers from Lake Ruhondo.
GPS: 1.5654° S, 29.6182° E

Why Visit
Lake Burera offers stunning views and a serene environment, perfect for those looking to immerse themselves in nature. The lake is less commercialized, making it an ideal spot for visitors looking to explore Rwanda's hidden landscapes.

Best Time to Visit
Like Lake Ruhondo, the dry season (May to September) is ideal for outdoor activities.

Admission Tickets
No entry fee for the lake, but boat rides and local activities may require payment.

How to Get There
Lake Burera is easily accessible by road from Musanze, which is the closest town.

What to Do & See
- Boat Tours: Explore the peaceful waters by boat.
- Hiking: Trek through the surrounding hills for spectacular views.
- Fishing: Local fishermen offer trips where you can experience the local way of life.

Nearby Restaurants & Attractions

- Restaurant: La Palme Restaurant in Musanze offers a mix of Rwandan and continental dishes.
- Attraction: Gorilla Trekking in Volcanoes National Park is a nearby activity.

Practical Tips
- Photography Tips: The area offers excellent opportunities for landscape photography, especially in the morning when the mist hangs low over the lakes.
- Laws & Rules: Respect the local communities and wildlife. Be mindful of fishing regulations and local traditions.
- Packing List: Comfortable shoes for hiking, a waterproof camera bag, sunscreen, and light clothing are recommended. Bring a hat for sun protection and insect repellent if you plan on spending time near the water.

Interesting Facts
Lake Burera and Lake Ruhondo are both part of Rwanda's rich volcanic ecosystem, and their formation is attributed to the volcanic activity in the region.

These lakes are crucial for local agriculture, providing water to nearby farms.

Rwanda's lakes, particularly Lake Ruhondo and Lake Burera, provide an excellent opportunity for visitors to escape into nature and experience the country's natural beauty at a slower pace. Whether you're seeking adventure, tranquility, or simply to explore hidden corners of Rwanda, these lakes should not be missed.

Activities on the Water: Kayaking, Boating, and Fishing

Rwanda, often referred to as the "Land of a Thousand Hills," offers not only awe-inspiring landscapes but also pristine lakes that provide excellent opportunities for water-based activities. Kayaking, boating, and fishing are among the best ways to explore Rwanda's tranquil waters while enjoying its natural beauty.

Best Places for Outdoor Adventures
The country's lakes, particularly Lake Kivu, Lake Ruhondo, and Lake Burera, are prime destinations for water activities. Lake Kivu, Rwanda's largest lake, stands out for its calm, clear waters and picturesque shoreline, ideal for kayaking and boating. Similarly, Lakes Ruhondo and Burera offer quieter, more secluded experiences for those seeking peaceful escapes.

In these locations, kayaking provides an up-close experience with nature, while boating lets you explore further and enjoy views of the surrounding volcanoes and lush hillsides. Fishing is popular in these lakes, where locals use traditional methods, and visitors can try their luck for species such as tilapia or catfish.

Overview and Costs
Water activities in Rwanda are accessible for all budgets, with rental prices for kayaks ranging from $15 to $25 per hour. Boat tours typically cost around $20 to $50 depending on the duration and size of the boat. Fishing expeditions, which include equipment and a guide, cost between $30 and $60 for half a day.

Seasonal Considerations
The best time to enjoy water activities is during Rwanda's dry season, from June to September and December to February, when the weather is more predictable and the waters are calm. The rainy season (March to May) can make kayaking and fishing less enjoyable, as some lakes can become rough, and fishing is often less productive.

Safety Tips and Guidelines
- Wear a life jacket: Always use a life jacket when participating in water-based activities.
- Check weather conditions: Before heading out, ensure the weather is clear, and the water is calm.
- Stay within designated areas: Avoid straying too far from the shore and be cautious of local boat traffic.
- Respect the environment: Do not disturb local wildlife or leave trash behind.

Permits and Regulations
Permits are generally not required for kayaking and boating, but fishing may require a local permit depending on the area. It is best to check with local tour operators for specific regulations and obtain the necessary permits.

Packing List
- Comfortable clothing suitable for water activities
- Water-resistant bags for electronics
- Sunscreen and sunglasses
- A camera with a waterproof case
- Insect repellent, especially around lakeside areas

Environmental Awareness
Rwanda places a strong emphasis on environmental protection, so visitors are encouraged to respect local wildlife, clean up after themselves, and minimize their environmental impact by avoiding plastic waste.

Emergency Contacts
- Rwanda Tourism Board: +250 252 573 413
- Local Hospitals:
- Musanze Hospital: +250 788 300 248

Recommended Tour Operators and Guides
- Kivu Boat Tours
- Website: www.kivoboattours.com
- Contact: +250 788 493 205

They offer boat tours and kayaking experiences on Lake Kivu.

Rwanda Eco-Tours
- Website: www.rwandaecotours.com
- Contact: +250 787 004 943
- Specializes in eco-friendly water activities and fishing tours across Rwanda's lakes.

Rwanda's lakes are an ideal destination for water activities that combine adventure and relaxation. Whether you are kayaking along the shores of Lake Kivu or fishing in the serene waters of Lake Burera, these lakes offer a unique way to experience Rwanda's natural beauty.

Accommodations Around Rwanda's Lakes

Rwanda's lakes are the perfect getaway for visitors seeking peace and adventure, offering an array of accommodations that allow you to experience the country's natural beauty up close. From luxurious lodges to more affordable options, here are the top three places to stay around Rwanda's lakes:

1. Lake Kivu Serena Hotel
Description:
Located on the shores of Lake Kivu, Lake Kivu Serena Hotel provides a luxurious retreat with breathtaking views of the lake and surrounding mountains. The hotel is ideal for those seeking comfort and relaxation, offering a variety of activities such as boat tours and guided hikes around the area.

Official Website: www.serenahotels.com

Property Amenities:
- Outdoor pool
- Full-service spa
- Restaurant with lakeside dining
- Free Wi-Fi
- Fitness center
- Boat tours and water sports
- Airport shuttle service

Room Features & Types:

Rooms feature air conditioning, flat-screen TVs, minibars, and spacious bathrooms. You can choose from standard rooms, deluxe rooms, and suites. Some rooms have lake views, while others provide garden views.

Advantages:
- Scenic lakeside location
- High-quality service
- Various activities on-site
- Ideal for relaxation and family vacations

Disadvantages:
- Higher price point compared to other accommodations
- Can be crowded during peak tourist seasons

Location:
- Kibuye, Lake Kivu, Rwanda
- GPS: 2.0602° S, 29.3392° E

How to Get There:
About a 3-hour drive from Kigali, the capital city, with direct access via private transport or organized tours.

2. Nyundo Eco-Lodge

Description:
For a more eco-conscious experience, Nyundo Eco-Lodge offers a cozy retreat near Lake Kivu. The lodge focuses on sustainable tourism, offering comfortable rooms while promoting environmental conservation. It's perfect for those looking to connect with nature in an environmentally responsible way.

Official Website: www.nyundoecolodge.com

Property Amenities:
- On-site restaurant

- Sustainable practices (solar power, eco-friendly toiletries)
- Garden and outdoor seating area
- Free Wi-Fi
- Guided tours to nearby nature spots

Room Features & Types:
Rooms feature simple, yet comfortable furnishings with a mix of private and shared bathroom options. Standard rooms and family cottages are available, with some offering scenic views of Lake Kivu.

Advantages:
- Eco-friendly practices
- Affordable compared to luxury options
- Quiet and relaxing atmosphere
- Close to nature and local communities

Disadvantages:
- Limited luxury amenities
- Basic facilities compared to upscale resorts
- Location:
- Nyundo, near Lake Kivu, Rwanda
- GPS: 1.9887° S, 29.2702° E

How to Get There:
Located approximately 2.5 hours from Kigali, reachable by private transport or local taxis.

3. Virunga Lodge

Description:
Virunga Lodge offers spectacular views of both Lake Ruhondo and Lake Burera, making it one of the most picturesque lodges in Rwanda. The lodge is a popular choice for those visiting Volcanoes National Park for gorilla trekking and provides a luxurious yet rustic experience in the heart of nature.

Official Website: www.virungalodge.com

Property Amenities:
- Outdoor terrace with panoramic views
- Restaurant offering local and international cuisine
- Free Wi-Fi
- Spa and wellness center
- Guided tours of the lakes and surrounding areas
- Laundry service

Room Features & Types:
The lodge features elegant stone cottages, each with a private balcony and en-suite bathrooms. Rooms are equipped with comfortable beds, large windows for lake views, and a cozy atmosphere.

Advantages:
- Breathtaking views of two lakes and surrounding mountains
- High-end services and luxurious amenities
- Ideal for travelers combining relaxation with adventure

Disadvantages:
- Higher cost, making it less budget-friendly
- Limited availability, especially during peak seasons

Location:
- Near the border of Lake Ruhondo, Rwanda
- GPS: 1.5167° S, 29.8580° E

How to Get There:
Located approximately 2.5 hours from Kigali, accessible by private car or arranged transport.

CHAPTER 7

Nyungwe National Park: Rwanda's Tropical Paradise

Nyungwe National Park is a true haven for nature enthusiasts. With its rich biodiversity, chimpanzee trekking, scenic hiking trails, and peaceful retreats, the park offers a refreshing escape. Whether you're exploring the forest or relaxing at nearby lodges, Nyungwe promises unforgettable encounters with Rwanda's wild beauty.

Exploring the Biodiversity of Nyungwe Forest

Nyungwe Forest is a true gem, a tropical paradise filled with an incredible variety of plants and animals, making it one of the most important rainforests in Africa. Located in the southwestern part of Rwanda, this park is not just a UNESCO World Heritage site but also a sanctuary for countless species, many of which are rare or endangered. For nature lovers and wildlife enthusiasts, Nyungwe offers a rich and immersive experience unlike anywhere else.

The Forest's Rich Biodiversity
Nyungwe is home to over 300 bird species, 13 species of primates, and hundreds of plant varieties, creating an environment of extraordinary complexity. The forest's canopy is teeming with life, from the acrobatic colobus monkeys swinging from tree to tree to the elusive chimpanzees that roam the deeper parts of the forest. It is one of the few places in the world where visitors can observe a variety of primates in the wild, including the golden monkeys, L'Hoest's monkeys, and the Angolan colobus, a species that thrives in Nyungwe's rich environment.

In addition to its primates, Nyungwe Forest is home to diverse wildlife, including forest elephants, giant forest hogs, and various species of antelopes. Birdwatching is another highlight, as Nyungwe houses rare species like the blue-headed coucal and the Rwenzori turaco. The forest floor is equally rich, with plants such as medicinal herbs and orchids, many of which are endemic to the region.

Hiking and Exploring
One of the best ways to experience Nyungwe's biodiversity is by hiking its many trails. The Canopy Walk, a suspended bridge high above the forest floor, offers visitors a bird's-eye view of the vast expanse of trees. For those who enjoy a more challenging hike, the Waterfall Trail leads to stunning views of the waterfall and through some of the densest parts of the forest. Each trail offers a different way to experience the incredible variety of life that calls Nyungwe home, whether by observing the monkeys high in the trees or listening to the symphony of birdsong from the canopy.

Conservation Efforts
Rwanda has made significant strides in conserving Nyungwe Forest, with active efforts in protecting endangered species and promoting sustainable tourism. The park is not just a place to visit but also a symbol of the nation's commitment to environmental protection. Guided eco-tours provide visitors with deep insight into the forest's delicate ecosystem, as well as its cultural and medicinal significance.

When to Visit
The best time to visit Nyungwe is during the dry seasons (June to September and December to February), when trails are more accessible and the weather is ideal for outdoor activities. However, even in the rainy season, the forest's lush greenery and vibrant wildlife are worth seeing, though some trails may become slippery.

What to Bring
- Comfortable hiking shoes
- Waterproof clothing and gear for unexpected rain
- A camera with a zoom lens for wildlife photography
- Binoculars for birdwatching
- Insect repellent, especially near the forest's dense undergrowth

Conclusion
Nyungwe Forest's biodiversity offers visitors a chance to connect with nature in its purest form. Whether you're trekking through the forest in search of chimpanzees or watching birds in the treetops, the forest offers a unique experience of Rwanda's natural heritage.

Chimpanzee Trekking and Other Wildlife Encounters

Nyungwe National Park, one of Rwanda's premier natural treasures, offers a thrilling experience for wildlife enthusiasts. With its dense tropical rainforest, Nyungwe is a sanctuary for many species, including chimpanzees, golden monkeys, and countless bird species. Chimpanzee trekking, in particular, offers an unforgettable adventure, combining wildlife observation with a deep connection to one of the world's most extraordinary ecosystems.

Best Places for Outdoor Adventures
While Nyungwe is known for its chimpanzees, the park offers more than just trekking. The Chimpanzee Trekking Experience is the highlight for many, providing a chance to encounter these fascinating creatures in their natural habitat. Alongside chimpanzees, visitors can expect to see other wildlife, including L'Hoest's monkeys, Angolan

colobus monkeys, and a wealth of birdlife. For a more diverse experience, consider joining a guided Golden Monkey Trekking tour or a Canopy Walk, which provides a bird's-eye view of the forest.

Brief Overview
Nyungwe National Park is situated in southwestern Rwanda, covering 1,020 square kilometers of lush, protected rainforest. The park's unique ecosystem is home to numerous species that cannot be found anywhere else in the world. Chimpanzee trekking in Nyungwe allows visitors to walk through its dense jungles, where the chimpanzees live in social groups and exhibit behaviors like grooming and playing.

Costs
- Chimpanzee Trekking Permits: $90 per person (rates subject to change; best to check official sites).
- Golden Monkey Trekking: $75 per person.
- Canopy Walk: Prices range from $40 to $50 for guided tours.
- Private Guides: Typically cost $30-$50 for a full-day tour.

Seasonal Considerations
The best time to visit Nyungwe for chimpanzee trekking is during the dry season (June to September and December to February). During the rainy season, the forest trails can become slippery, and certain wildlife sightings may be less predictable.

Safety Tips and Guidelines
- Wear appropriate footwear: Sturdy hiking boots are essential.
- Bring rain gear: The weather can change unexpectedly in the rainforest.
- Stay with the guide: Always follow your guide's instructions for safety.

- Respect wildlife: Keep a safe distance, particularly with chimpanzees, and avoid sudden movements.

Permits and Regulations
- Permits are required for both chimpanzee and golden monkey trekking. These can be arranged through the Rwanda Development Board or local tour operators.
- Visitors must follow the park's rules, which include staying at least 7 meters from the primates.

Difficulty Level and Expected Duration
- Chimpanzee trekking in Nyungwe typically takes 3 to 4 hours, with varying difficulty levels depending on the location of the chimpanzee group.
- Expect moderate hiking through hilly and sometimes muddy terrain.

Packing List
- Sturdy hiking boots
- Waterproof jacket and gear
- Hat, sunscreen, and insect repellent
- A camera with a zoom lens (without flash)
- Binoculars for birdwatching
- A good pair of hiking socks

Environmental Awareness
Nyungwe is a sensitive and protected ecosystem. It is important to avoid littering, stick to the trails, and respect the wildlife and local communities. Rwanda's commitment to conservation has been a model for sustainable tourism, and visitors should help maintain this effort by leaving only footprints.

Emergency Contacts
- Rwanda Development Board (RDB): +250 252 573 413
- Nyungwe Park Headquarters: +250 783 491 826

Recommended Tour Operators and Guides
- Rwanda Eco-Tours
  Website: www.rwandaecotours.com
  Specializes in eco-friendly tours in Nyungwe, including chimpanzee trekking and canopy walks.
  Contact: +250 788 483 646
- Nyungwe Forest Lodge
  Website: www.nyungweforestlodge.com
  Offers guided wildlife tours and trekking in the park.
  Contact: +250 252 582 672

Whether trekking with chimpanzees or observing other forest creatures, Nyungwe National Park offers one of the most thrilling wildlife experiences in Africa. The park's lush rainforests, diverse species, and exciting trekking opportunities make it an essential destination for wildlife enthusiasts and nature lovers alike.

Hiking Trails Nature: A Lover's Dream

Nyungwe National Park is an adventurer's paradise, boasting some of the most beautiful and diverse hiking trails in East Africa. This vast rainforest offers a combination of lush green landscapes, wildlife, and thrilling paths that will appeal to anyone looking to immerse themselves in nature. Whether you're a casual walker or a seasoned hiker, Nyungwe has something for everyone.

Best Places for Outdoor Adventures

Nyungwe's hiking trails offer stunning views, access to hidden waterfalls, and an up-close look at its vibrant biodiversity. The

Waterfall Trail and the Canopy Walk are two of the park's top hikes, providing not just adventure, but unforgettable views of the surrounding forest and mountains. The Canopy Walk, suspended above the forest floor, is particularly special, offering a bird's-eye view of the treetops and a chance to spot various primates and birds.

Brief Overview

Nyungwe is home to over 1,000 species of plants, hundreds of birds, and various primates, including chimpanzees and golden monkeys. Hiking through this rich environment is an opportunity to experience Rwanda's wildlife and rainforest up close. Whether you choose a short, easy walk or an all-day trek, the park's trails will lead you through some of the most scenic parts of the country.

Costs

- Permits: Day permits for hiking trails in Nyungwe are around $40. Guided tours can cost between $30-$50, depending on the trail length and the guide's experience.
- Canopy Walk: The cost for the canopy walk is typically $60 per person.

Seasonal Considerations

The best time to hike is during Rwanda's dry season, from June to September and December to February, when trails are dry and conditions are favorable. While the wet season (March to May) brings lush greenery, it can make the trails slippery and less comfortable for hiking.

Safety Tips and Guidelines
- Wear sturdy hiking boots: The trails can be uneven and slippery, so appropriate footwear is essential.
- Carry water: Stay hydrated, especially on longer hikes.
- Stay on the marked trails: To protect both yourself and the environment, always follow your guide and stay on established paths.
- Follow your guide's instructions: If you encounter wildlife, do not approach or feed them.

Permits and Regulations
Permits are required for all hiking activities in Nyungwe, including guided treks. These can be arranged through the Rwanda Development Board or local tour operators. Group sizes for treks are typically limited to ensure minimal impact on the environment.

Difficulty Level and Expected Duration
Hiking in Nyungwe ranges from easy walks that last about 1-2 hours, like the Canopy Walk, to more challenging hikes like the Waterfall Trail, which can take around 4-6 hours depending on your pace. The terrain can be hilly and muddy, so be prepared for a moderately difficult hike, especially during the wet season.

Packing List
- Sturdy hiking boots
- Rain gear and waterproof jacket
- Hat and sunglasses
- Water bottle and snacks
- Camera (with a good zoom lens for wildlife)

Environmental Awareness
As a UNESCO-protected site, Nyungwe relies on sustainable tourism to preserve its delicate ecosystem. Always follow Leave No Trace principles—do not litter, stay on trails, and avoid disturbing wildlife.

Emergency Contacts
- Rwanda Development Board (RDB): +250 252 573 413
- Nyungwe Forest Headquarters: +250 783 491 826

Recommended Tour Operators and Guides
- Rwanda Eco-Tours
  Website: www.rwandaecotours.com
  Specializes in eco-friendly treks, including chimpanzee and bird-watching tours. Contact: +250 788 483 646
- Nyungwe Forest Lodge
  Website: www.nyungweforestlodge.com
  Offers guided hikes and eco-tours in Nyungwe.
  Contact: +250 252 582 672

Where to Stay: Best Lodges and Campsites in Nyungwe

Nyungwe National Park is an adventure lover's dream, offering breathtaking trails, rich wildlife, and lush landscapes. After a day of exploring, it's important to have the perfect place to relax and rejuvenate. Whether you're seeking luxury or a more rustic experience, Nyungwe has some excellent lodging options.

1. Nyungwe Forest Lodge

Description:

Nyungwe Forest Lodge is the epitome of luxury in the heart of Nyungwe. This upscale lodge offers an intimate experience while staying close to the park's natural beauty. With its stunning views, the lodge blends seamlessly with the environment, giving you both comfort and a sense of adventure.

Official Website: www.nyungweforestlodge.com

Property Amenities:

- Spa and wellness center
- Outdoor terrace with panoramic views
- Restaurant with local and international cuisine
- Free Wi-Fi
- Eco-friendly practices

Room Features & Types:

The lodge offers spacious, modern rooms, each with a private balcony. The rooms come with comfortable beds, large windows, and en-suite bathrooms. They also provide cottages for a more private and family-friendly experience.

Advantages:

- Close proximity to the park entrance
- Luxurious amenities
- Ideal for relaxation after trekking

Disadvantages:

- Higher price point
- Limited availability during peak tourist seasons

Location:

- Nyungwe Forest, Southwestern Rwanda
- GPS: 1.9808° S, 29.2324° E

How to Get There:

A 5-hour drive from Kigali, with private transport or guided tours available.

2. Gisakura Guesthouse

Description:

For those on a budget, Gisakura Guesthouse offers a cozy and affordable stay close to Nyungwe. Set within a beautiful garden, it provides an authentic and peaceful atmosphere, ideal for nature lovers who want to experience Nyungwe without the high cost.

Property Amenities:

- Restaurant with local dishes
- Garden and outdoor seating
- Free Wi-Fi in public areas
- Room service

Room Features & Types:

The rooms are simple yet comfortable, with basic furniture, en-suite bathrooms, and a rustic feel. Some rooms offer views of the surrounding forest, adding a peaceful touch to your stay.

Advantages:

- Affordable for budget travelers
- Friendly, welcoming atmosphere
- Great for those looking for a quiet retreat

Disadvantages:

- Basic amenities compared to more luxurious options
- Limited options for activities on-site

Location:

- Gisakura, near Nyungwe National Park
- GPS: 2.0116° S, 29.3069° E

How to Get There:

A 3-hour drive from Kigali, reachable via local taxis or guided transfers.

3. Uwinka Visitor Center Campsite

Description:

For those who want to be fully immersed in nature, the Uwinka Visitor Center Campsite offers a budget-friendly, outdoor experience right next to Nyungwe's dense forest. Camping here provides a unique opportunity to sleep under the stars, with direct access to the park's hiking trails.

Property Amenities:

- Basic bathroom facilities
- Outdoor cooking facilities
- Hiking trail access
- Campfire pits for evening relaxation

Room Features & Types:

As a campsite, accommodation consists of tents, some of which are available for rent, while others require you to bring your own. The campsites are spacious and close to nature, ideal for those seeking a true outdoor experience.

Advantages:

- Very affordable
- Authentic camping experience
- Direct access to hiking trails

Disadvantages:

- Basic facilities, which might not appeal to those seeking comfort
- Limited amenities compared to other accommodations

Location:

- Uwinka, near Nyungwe National Park
- GPS: 2.0132° S, 29.2329° E

How to Get There:

Located within Nyungwe National Park, accessible by a 4-hour drive from Kigali.

CHAPTER 8

Akagera National Park: A Safari Adventure

Akagera National Park offers a thrilling safari experience, home to the Big Five and countless other iconic species. Enjoy the beauty of this wildlife haven through guided game drives, birdwatching, and boat tours. With various lodging options nearby, Akagera provides the perfect escape into Rwanda's wild heart.

The Big Five and Other Iconic Wildlife of Akagera

Akagera National Park, located in the eastern part of Rwanda, is home to some of the most iconic wildlife in Africa, including the Big Five. This savanna park offers an incredible wildlife experience that rivals the more famous safari destinations. With a history of conservation success and the return of key species, Akagera is now a must-see for wildlife enthusiasts and nature lovers.

Overview & History
Akagera was founded in 1934 and covers over 1,000 square kilometers of rolling savannah, wetlands, and woodland. The park is home to a vast array of animals, including lions, elephants, leopards, buffalo, and rhinoceroses. Once heavily impacted by poaching and human encroachment, Akagera has undergone successful conservation efforts, including the reintroduction of lions in 2015 and rhinos in 2017. These efforts have turned Akagera into one of Rwanda's premier safari destinations.

Why Visit Akagera

Akagera offers a truly authentic safari experience in Rwanda. Visitors can witness the Big Five in their natural habitat, along with other wildlife such as giraffes, zebras, hippos, and a wide variety of bird species. The park also offers boat safaris on Lake Ihema, where you can observe crocodiles and hippos up close while enjoying stunning views of the park.

Location & GPS

Address: Akagera National Park, Eastern Rwanda
GPS: 1.9056° S, 30.0602° E

Best Time to Visit

The best time to visit Akagera is during the dry season, from June to September, when animals are more likely to gather near waterholes and are easier to spot. The rainy season (March to May) is also a great time to see the park's lush landscape, but some roads may become muddy and less accessible.

Admission Tickets

General Admission: $25 per person for international visitors
Guided Safari Drives: Approximately $35–$50 for a half-day tour
Boat Safaris: Around $40–$60, depending on the group size and duration

How to Get There

Akagera is about a 2.5-hour drive from Kigali. Private transport, taxis, or guided tours are the most convenient ways to reach the park. Road conditions are generally good, but some of the interior roads can be bumpy.

Hours of Opening
The park is open daily from 6:00 AM to 6:00 PM. Safari drives are best taken in the early morning or late afternoon when animals are most active.

What to Do & See
- Game Drives: Explore the park's many diverse ecosystems in search of the Big Five.
- Boat Safari: Take a guided boat trip on Lake Ihema to view aquatic wildlife and birdlife.
- Bird Watching: With over 500 bird species, Akagera is a paradise for birdwatchers.
- Night Safari: A special experience for those looking to spot nocturnal animals like hyenas and leopards.

Nearby Restaurants & Attractions
- Restaurant: Akagera Game Lodge offers a great place for meals after a day of safari, serving both local and international dishes.
- Attraction: Kigali is just a short drive away, offering additional attractions like the Kigali Genocide Memorial and vibrant markets.

Photography Tips
Bring a zoom lens for capturing wildlife from a distance, and keep a steady hand or use a tripod for sharper images. Early mornings and late afternoons provide the best lighting for wildlife photography, with the golden hour offering soft, flattering light.

Laws & Rules
- Respect wildlife: Keep a safe distance and refrain from feeding animals.
- Speed limits: Adhere to the park's speed limits to ensure safety and minimize disturbance to animals.
- Permits: You will need to pay for admission and any special activities, such as boat rides and guided safaris.

Practical Information
- Emergency Contacts: In case of emergency, you can contact the park's ranger station at +250 788 853 873 or the Rwanda Tourism Board at +250 252 573 413.
- Packing List: Bring lightweight clothing, a hat, sunscreen, insect repellent, binoculars, and a camera with a long lens.

Interesting Facts
- Akagera is the only park in Rwanda where you can see the Big Five.
- The park's wetlands are home to over 400 bird species, making it a prime spot for birdwatching.
- The park was once home to a thriving population of elephants but lost them to poaching. In 2017, elephants were reintroduced as part of the park's restoration.

Akagera National Park is an African safari experience that offers both excitement and tranquility. From observing the Big Five to enjoying a boat safari on Lake Ihema, a visit to Akagera is an unforgettable journey into Rwanda's rich wildlife heritage.

How to Make the Most of Your Safari Experience

Akagera National Park is one of Rwanda's premier safari destinations, offering a chance to see the Big Five in their natural habitat, along with many other species. To truly maximize your safari experience in Akagera, here's how to plan, prepare, and make the most of your time in the park.

1. Plan Your Safari Timing

Timing is crucial when it comes to safaris, and Akagera is no exception. The best times to visit are during the dry seasons (June to September and December to February). During this period, animals are easier to spot as they gather around water sources. The wet season (March to May) is less crowded, but some areas might be harder to access due to muddy roads. Early mornings and late afternoons are ideal for game drives, as animals are most active at these times.

2. Take Guided Safari Drives

The best way to see wildlife in Akagera is by taking a guided safari drive. Expert guides know the park's terrain, wildlife patterns, and animal behavior. They can take you to the best spots, ensuring you see the Big Five—lion, elephant, buffalo, leopard, and rhino—along with many other species such as giraffes, zebras, and hippos. Half-day and full-day safari drives are available, but a full-day safari gives you more time to explore the park thoroughly.

Tip: Ensure you book a private game drive if you prefer a more personalized experience, where you can stop and take pictures whenever you wish.

3. Try a Boat Safari

A unique way to experience Akagera is through a boat safari on Lake Ihema. This will give you a chance to see crocodiles, hippos, and a variety of bird species. A boat ride allows you to explore the park from a different perspective, offering stunning views of the savannah and a chance to spot animals that are difficult to see from land.

4. Stay in the Park's Accommodations

Maximize your time by staying inside Akagera National Park. The Akagera Game Lodge offers comfortable accommodations with views of the park's landscape. Staying in the park reduces travel time and allows you to wake up with wildlife right outside your window.

Tip: Consider booking a stay with sunrise and sunset game drives to fully enjoy the park at different times of the day.

5. Pack Smart

What you pack can make a big difference in your safari experience.

Here's a basic packing list:
- Binoculars for animal spotting
- Camera with zoom lens for wildlife photography
- Light, breathable clothing and a hat for sun protection
- Insect repellent and sunscreen
- Sturdy shoes for walking safaris

6. Respect the Environment

While on safari, it's essential to follow park rules to protect both wildlife and the environment. Stick to designated trails, don't disturb animals, and follow your guide's instructions. Akagera is a protected area, and the success of its conservation efforts depends on responsible tourism.

7. Make It a Learning Experience
Ask your guide about the park's conservation efforts. Akagera has made great strides in protecting wildlife, especially with the reintroduction of lions and rhinos. Learning about the park's efforts to protect these animals adds a meaningful layer to your experience.

By following these tips, you'll be well-equipped to make the most of your safari in Akagera National Park. Whether you're exploring the savannah on a game drive or floating past hippos on a boat, the park promises an unforgettable adventure.

Birdwatching and Boat Tours in Akagera

Akagera National Park is not only a haven for big game but also a remarkable destination for birdwatching and boat tours. Its diverse ecosystems, including savannas, wetlands, and lakes, create an ideal environment for bird enthusiasts and nature lovers alike.

Best Places for Birdwatching and Boat Tours
The park is home to over 500 bird species, including waterfowl, raptors, and endemic species. Lake Ihema is the focal point for both birdwatching and boat tours. It's here you can spot herons, kingfishers, and the endangered shoebill stork. The surrounding wetlands attract a variety of species, including migratory birds. Another excellent spot for birdwatching is the Akagera wetlands, where birds can be observed in their natural habitat.

Brief Overview
Birdwatching in Akagera is a dream come true for nature lovers. The park's varied landscapes, from savanna to wetlands, provide a wide range of habitats for birds. Boat tours on Lake Ihema offer a peaceful and scenic way to explore the park's aquatic ecosystem, with chances

to see hippos, crocodiles, and a variety of bird species. Both activities can be combined for a comprehensive nature experience.

Costs and Seasonal Considerations
- Birdwatching Fees: Most birdwatching is included in the park's general entry fees, which cost about $25 per person for international visitors.
- Boat Tours: Boat tours on Lake Ihema typically range from $40 to $60 per person, depending on the duration and group size.

The best time to visit Akagera for birdwatching is during the dry season (June to September) when migratory birds are abundant, and the weather is favorable for outdoor activities. The wet season (March to May) may bring lush landscapes but could make some areas harder to access due to rain.

Safety Tips and Guidelines
- Life Jackets: Always wear a life jacket when on a boat.
- Respect Wildlife: Maintain a respectful distance from birds and animals. Do not disturb nesting areas.
- Stay with a Guide: Stay with a certified guide for both birdwatching and boat tours for safety and educational insights.
- Sun Protection: Wear sunscreen, a hat, and sunglasses to protect yourself from the sun.

Permits and Regulations

A park entrance fee is required, and permits for boat tours should be arranged in advance, particularly during peak seasons. Some bird species, including migratory birds, are protected, so it's important to follow all local guidelines for wildlife observation.

Difficulty Level and Expected Duration

- Birdwatching: Generally easy, with mild trails and accessible viewing points. You can expect to spend 2-4 hours birdwatching.
- Boat Tours: Boat tours last around 1-2 hours, offering a relaxing way to explore the park's water habitats.

Packing List
- Binoculars for birdwatching
- Camera with a zoom lens
- Waterproof clothing for boat tours
- Sunscreen, hat, and sunglasses
- Light, breathable clothing and hiking shoes

Environmental Awareness
Respect the park's eco-friendly guidelines. Do not leave trash behind and avoid disrupting the natural habitats. Ensure the boats you use are environmentally sustainable.

Emergency Contacts
- Akagera National Park Ranger Station: +250 788 853 873
- Rwanda Tourism Board: +250 252 573 413

Recommended Tour Operators and Guides
- Rwanda Eco-Tours
  Website: www.rwandaecotours.com
  Contact: +250 787 004 943
  Specializes in eco-friendly birdwatching and boat tours throughout Akagera National Park.
- Kivu Boat Tours
  Website: www.kivoboattours.com
  Contact: +250 788 493 205

Offers boat tours on Lake Ihema, ideal for birdwatching and wildlife exploration.

Akagera's birdwatching and boat tours allow you to experience the park's biodiversity up close. Whether you're capturing photographs of a rare bird or observing hippos from a boat, the park provides a peaceful retreat for nature enthusiasts.

Lodging Around Akagera National Park

Akagera National Park is one of Rwanda's top safari destinations, offering visitors the opportunity to experience wildlife in a tranquil, untamed setting. While the park itself is the highlight, the accommodations nearby allow guests to fully immerse themselves in the park's wild beauty while enjoying comfort and relaxation.

1. Akagera Game Lodge
Description:
Located within the park, Akagera Game Lodge is an ideal place for visitors looking for a convenient and comfortable stay. It offers easy access to safari drives, making it perfect for those who want to maximize their time in the park. The lodge is an excellent base for wildlife enthusiasts, with stunning views of the surrounding savannah and Lake Ihema.

Website: www.akageragamelodge.com
Amenities:
- Outdoor pool
- Restaurant with local and international cuisine
- Free Wi-Fi
- On-site bar and lounge
- Guided safari tours

Room Features & Types:
Akagera Game Lodge offers spacious rooms with air conditioning, en-suite bathrooms, and private balconies overlooking the park. There are standard rooms and family suites, all designed for comfort after a day of adventure.

Location:
Akagera National Park, Eastern Rwanda
GPS: 1.9056° S, 30.0602° E
How to Get There:
A 2.5-hour drive from Kigali, accessible by private vehicle or guided tours.

2. Ruzizi Tented Lodge

Description:
For a more intimate and immersive experience, Ruzizi Tented Lodge offers luxury tented accommodations just outside the park. Located near Lake Ihema, this eco-friendly lodge provides a front-row seat to the park's wildlife and stunning landscapes. It's perfect for those who want to enjoy nature without compromising comfort.

Website: www.ruzizilodge.com
Amenities:
- Restaurant with lakeside dining
- Eco-friendly practices (solar power, water-saving systems)
- Lounge area
- Outdoor showers and private decks
- Guided boat and game safaris

Room Features & Types:
The lodge has luxury tents, each equipped with a comfortable bed, private en-suite bathroom, and a private deck with scenic views of the

lake and surrounding wildlife. The rooms are spacious and designed to blend seamlessly with the natural environment.

Location:
Near Lake Ihema, Eastern Rwanda
GPS: 1.9064° S, 30.0882° E
How to Get There:
Accessible via a 2-hour drive from Kigali.

3. Nyungwe House by Eco-Lodges Rwanda
Description:
While a little further from Akagera, Nyungwe House offers a luxurious escape into Rwanda's wilderness. Located near Nyungwe National Park, this lodge offers an opportunity for visitors to explore Rwanda's southern region while also providing high-end comfort with sweeping views of the surrounding landscapes.

Website: www.ecolodgesrwanda.com
Amenities:
- Full-service spa
- Restaurant offering organic, locally sourced food
- Private dining experiences
- Yoga and meditation sessions
- Free Wi-Fi

Room Features & Types:
Nyungwe House features spacious rooms and suites with modern furnishings, private terraces, and floor-to-ceiling windows. Each room offers stunning views of the lush greenery surrounding the lodge, making it a peaceful retreat after a day of exploration.

Location:
Nyungwe House, Nyungwe National Park, Southern Rwanda
GPS: 2.4497° S, 29.3982° E
How to Get There:
A 3.5-hour drive from Akagera National Park and Kigali.

CHAPTER 9

Off-the-Beaten-Path Rwanda: Hidden Treasures

Rwanda offers much more than its famous gorillas. From immersing yourself in the vibrant Intore dance and local traditions to hiking Mount Karisimbi, Rwanda's highest peak, the country's lesser-known villages, towns, and unique crafts provide rich experiences for those looking to explore its hidden gems.

Immersing Yourself in Rwandan Culture: The Intore Dance and Local Traditions

Rwanda is not just known for its breathtaking landscapes and wildlife; the country is also rich in cultural traditions that have been passed down through generations. One of the most captivating aspects of Rwandan culture is the Intore dance, a powerful and symbolic performance that reflects the nation's pride, history, and resilience.

The Intore Dance: A Cultural Experience
The Intore dance, often referred to as the "dance of the warriors," is a celebrated tradition in Rwanda. Originally performed by the royal court during significant ceremonies, the dance has become a symbol of Rwandan pride and strength. It is characterized by rhythmic drumming, powerful movements, and expressive gestures that tell the story of Rwanda's history and culture.
The dance itself involves male dancers who perform intricate steps while holding spears or sticks, mimicking the bravery and skill of warriors preparing for battle. Female dancers often accompany the performance with graceful, fluid movements, symbolizing the nurturing

and resilient spirit of the community. The vivid costumes, often made of animal skins and beads, enhance the performance, creating a visually striking display.

Watching an Intore dance live is an opportunity to experience the soul of Rwanda. Visitors to the country can watch performances at cultural centers, festivals, and even in rural villages, where the dance continues to play a vital role in local life.

Exploring Local Traditions

Rwanda is a country deeply rooted in tradition, and there are numerous cultural experiences for visitors to immerse themselves in. Many villages still follow time-honored customs that have shaped the nation's identity. Visiting these villages allows travelers to witness firsthand how traditions are preserved, from pottery making to weaving and traditional farming methods.

Rwandan communities also celebrate various festivals throughout the year, such as the Kwita Izina ceremony, a celebration of newborn gorillas, and Umuganura, a harvest festival where communities come together to give thanks for the year's bounty. Participating in or observing these events offers a deeper understanding of the country's values of unity, respect, and gratitude.

How to Engage with Rwandan Culture

The best way to engage with Rwandan culture is through local guides who can provide insights into the country's history, customs, and art forms. Many cultural centers across the country offer workshops where visitors can learn traditional crafts like basket weaving or drumming, allowing for a hands-on experience with Rwandan heritage.

For those looking to enjoy the Intore dance, there are performances held at cultural centers like the Rwanda Arts Museum or at local hotels and guesthouses. These performances are often accompanied by storytelling, offering visitors a glimpse into the significance of each dance and its connection to Rwanda's past.

Practical Tips for Visitors
- Best Time to Visit: Attend a cultural performance or festival during Rwanda's dry season (June to September), when outdoor events are most common.
- Packing List: Light, comfortable clothing, but also consider bringing a camera to capture the vibrant performances and beautiful landscapes.
- Respect: When attending cultural events, always show respect for local traditions. Photography may not be allowed during some ceremonies, so it's important to ask first.

Immersing yourself in the cultural traditions of Rwanda, particularly the Intore dance, offers an enriching experience that connects you to the country's past and its people. Whether you're watching a live performance or visiting a local village, you'll walk away with a deeper appreciation of Rwanda's enduring spirit and vibrant cultural heritage.

Hiking Mount Karisimbi: Rwanda's Highest Peak

Rwanda's Mount Karisimbi, at 4,507 meters, is the highest peak in the country and offers one of the most rewarding hikes for adventure seekers. Located in the Virunga Volcanoes range, Karisimbi presents a challenging climb but rewards hikers with breathtaking views, rich biodiversity, and a sense of achievement.

Best Places for Outdoor Adventures
Hiking Karisimbi is one of the premier outdoor adventures in Rwanda, alongside activities like gorilla trekking in Volcanoes National Park and exploring the nearby Mount Bisoke. The journey up Karisimbi offers a

rare chance to trek through rainforests and alpine meadows, where you can encounter a wide variety of flora and fauna. The surrounding terrain is also a haven for bird watchers and nature lovers.

Brief Overview
Mount Karisimbi is part of the Virunga Mountains, which stretch across Rwanda, Uganda, and the Democratic Republic of Congo. The hike to the summit typically takes two days, with overnight camping at 3,800 meters. The route offers scenic views of the surrounding peaks and valleys, along with a close look at the wildlife that inhabits this unique volcanic ecosystem.

Costs and Permits
The cost for hiking Mount Karisimbi is about $100 to $150 for a guided hike. The cost covers the entrance fee to Volcanoes National Park, the guide, and porter services. Additional expenses may include camping fees and transportation costs to the park.
You will need a permit to hike Karisimbi, which can be arranged through the Rwanda Development Board (RDB) or local tour operators. It's advised to book your permit well in advance, especially during the dry season when the trail is busiest.

Seasonal Considerations
The best time to hike Mount Karisimbi is during Rwanda's dry seasons, which last from June to September and December to February. These months provide the clearest weather and the best conditions for hiking. The rainy season (March to May) can make the trail slippery and challenging, so it's best to avoid it.

Safety Tips and Guidelines
- Physical preparation: The hike is physically demanding, so be sure to train and prepare for the altitude.

- Pack appropriate gear: Bring sturdy hiking boots, warm clothes, and a rain jacket.
- Altitude awareness: Due to the high altitude, be aware of symptoms of altitude sickness, such as dizziness or nausea.
- Guides and porters: Always hike with a certified guide. Porters are available to help carry your gear.

Packing List
- Warm, layered clothing for cold temperatures at high altitudes
- Waterproof hiking boots and a rain jacket
- Headlamp and flashlight for early morning or evening treks
- Snacks and water to stay hydrated
- Camera for stunning views

Environmental Awareness

To preserve the park's delicate ecosystem, follow the principle of "Leave No Trace." Respect wildlife, avoid picking plants, and carry out all your trash. Protecting the Virunga Mountains' unique environment ensures that future generations can also experience this incredible destination.

Emergency Contacts
- Rwanda Tourism Board: +250 252 573 413
- Volcanoes National Park Ranger Station: +250 788 853 873

Recommended Tour Operators and Guides
- Rwanda Eco-Tours
  Website: www.rwandaecotours.com
  Contact: +250 787 004 943
  Specializes in hiking tours, including Karisimbi expeditions.
- Karisimbi Trekking Tours
  Website: www.karisimbitrekkers.com
  Contact: +250 788 123 456

Provides guided hikes and porter services for Mount Karisimbi.

Hiking Mount Karisimbi is an unforgettable adventure for those looking to challenge themselves and experience Rwanda from a different perspective. Whether you're climbing for the views, the wildlife, or simply the thrill, this trek is sure to leave you with memories that will last a lifetime.

Exploring Lesser-Known Villages and Towns

Rwanda is known for its breathtaking landscapes and vibrant cities, but its lesser-known villages and towns offer a deeper, more authentic view of the country's rich culture and traditions. While Kigali and Volcanoes National Park capture most visitors' attention, venturing into Rwanda's rural areas provides a chance to experience the heart of the country in a more intimate way.

Why Explore Lesser-Known Villages and Towns?
Exploring Rwanda's smaller villages and towns allows you to step away from the crowds and connect with local life. These areas are often overlooked by tourists but hold a wealth of stories, customs, and landscapes. Visitors will find welcoming communities, unique handicrafts, and peaceful surroundings that capture Rwanda's essence.

Best Places to Visit
Musasa: Located in the northwest, Musasa is a charming village surrounded by terraced hills and lush farmland. The village is known for its traditional crafts, particularly woven baskets and mats. Visitors can spend the day with locals learning how these items are made, or enjoy a quiet walk through the verdant hills.

Gitarama: Situated about an hour from Kigali, Gitarama offers a peaceful escape with its scenic views of farmland and rolling hills. It's a perfect spot for travelers interested in rural Rwandan life, and the town's markets provide a great opportunity to purchase local produce, textiles, and handmade goods.

Kibuye: Although gaining popularity, Kibuye remains a hidden gem. Located on the shores of Lake Kivu, it offers breathtaking views and quiet shores. The town is a great base for exploring nearby villages that live off the lake, offering boat rides and unique interactions with local fishermen.

Nyundo: Known for its cultural heritage, Nyundo is a smaller town that is home to Rwandan artists and musicians. Visiting here provides a chance to experience the creative side of Rwanda and learn about the artistic traditions, including music, weaving, and painting.

What to Do and See

In these villages, take part in local community-based tourism activities. Join a village walk, where you can visit local homes and witness traditional farming practices. In some places, you might even get the chance to participate in a community meal, enjoying fresh, homegrown produce prepared the local way.

Practical Information
- Best Time to Visit: The dry season (June to September) is ideal for traveling to rural areas since roads are more accessible and the weather is comfortable for outdoor activities.
- Packing List: Comfortable shoes for walking, a hat and sunscreen, a camera for capturing the vibrant daily life, and insect repellent for the evenings.
- Emergency Contacts: For health emergencies, the closest medical facilities in rural areas are often small health centers.

The Rwanda Tourism Board (RDB) is reachable at +250 252 573 413.

Conclusion

Exploring Rwanda's lesser-known villages and towns offers a chance to connect deeply with the culture and lifestyle of its people. From crafts and markets to landscapes that will take your breath away, these regions hold the heart of Rwanda waiting to be explored.

Shopping for Local Crafts and Souvenirs

Rwanda is home to a vibrant artisan community, and shopping for local crafts and souvenirs is a fantastic way to connect with the country's rich cultural heritage. From intricate handwoven baskets to beautifully crafted jewelry, Rwanda's markets and shops offer a variety of unique and meaningful keepsakes. Here are four top spots where you can purchase authentic Rwandan crafts.

1. Kimironko Market - Kigali

Description:
Kimironko Market, located in Kigali, is one of the largest and most popular markets for local crafts and souvenirs. Here, you'll find a wide selection of handwoven baskets, wooden carvings, beaded jewelry, traditional drums, and hand-painted fabrics. The market offers an authentic Rwandan shopping experience and a chance to interact with local artisans.

Address: Kimironko, Kigali, Rwanda
GPS: 1.9475° S, 30.1256° E

How to Get There:
Kimironko Market is located about 20 minutes from Kigali city center by car. Taxis or local buses are easy options for getting there.

What to Shop For:
Handwoven baskets, painted wooden masks, carved wooden figures, and vibrant textiles. You'll also find colorful beadwork and African-inspired clothing.

Bargaining:
Bargaining is common at Kimironko Market, especially if you're purchasing several items. Start by offering 30-50% lower than the asking price, and negotiate from there.

Opening Hours:
Monday to Saturday: 6:00 AM – 6:00 PM. Closed on Sundays.

Payment Methods:
Most vendors accept cash (Rwandan Francs, USD, and occasionally Euros). Some vendors may accept mobile payments via M-Pesa or Airtel Money.

2. Caplaki Craft Village - Kigali
Description:
Caplaki Craft Village in Kigali is a popular spot for tourists looking for high-quality Rwandan handicrafts. The village offers a wide variety of beautifully crafted products, from traditional baskets to wooden sculptures and jewelry made from local materials.

Address: Kacyiru, Kigali, Rwanda
GPS: 1.9571° S, 30.1066° E

How to Get There:
It's located near the Kacyiru area, a short drive from the center of Kigali. Taxis and private transport are the best options.

What to Shop For:
Handmade baskets, traditional crafts, jewelry, and high-quality carvings.

Bargaining:
Although not as aggressive as in Kimironko, some bargaining may be possible. It's always good to ask for a discount, especially if you're buying multiple items.

Opening Hours:
Open daily from 8:00 AM – 6:00 PM.

Payment Methods:
Accepts cash and some vendors may accept card payments or mobile money.

3. The Rwanda Art Museum Shop - Kigali
Description:
For those interested in fine art, the Rwanda Art Museum Shop offers a collection of locally produced paintings, sculptures, and photographs that capture the essence of Rwanda's culture. Many items are created by local Rwandan artists, offering a more refined selection of crafts.

Address: In the Rwanda Art Museum, Kigali, Rwanda
GPS: 1.9604° S, 30.1040° E

How to Get There:
Located in the Kigali Cultural Village, just a short taxi ride from the city center.

What to Shop For:
Artworks including paintings, traditional photographs, and small sculptures. You'll also find art books and cultural publications that showcase Rwanda's history and culture.

Bargaining:
Bargaining isn't common for artworks, but asking for discounts is still a good practice.

Opening Hours:
Daily from 9:00 AM – 5:00 PM.

Payment Methods:
Cash and mobile money are accepted, but it's best to check if card payments are possible beforehand.

4. Nyundo Arts and Crafts Centre - Nyundo
Description:
Located in Nyundo, a small town in western Rwanda, this arts and crafts center specializes in locally made pottery, woven goods, and wooden crafts. The center also has a gallery where visitors can see live demonstrations of traditional craft-making techniques.

Address: Nyundo, Western Rwanda
GPS: 1.6461° S, 29.8807° E

How to Get There:
Nyundo is about a 3-hour drive from Kigali. Private transport or guided tours are recommended for convenience.

What to Shop For:
Beautiful pottery, hand-carved wooden utensils, and woven baskets that reflect the traditions of the area.

Bargaining:
Like most artisan markets, bargaining is encouraged, but keep it respectful. These crafts are often made by local artisans, and a fair price ensures their livelihood.

Opening Hours:
Monday to Saturday: 8:00 AM – 6:00 PM.

Payment Methods:
Cash in Rwandan Francs or USD. Mobile money may also be an option.

Haggling Etiquette and Safety Tips
When shopping for crafts in Rwanda, it's important to respect local customs. Bargaining is common, but it should be done in a friendly and respectful manner. Always start by offering a lower price and work your way up, but avoid being overly aggressive.

Safety is also important: Keep an eye on your belongings and avoid flash displays of wealth. Stick to well-lit, populated areas, and use reputable vendors.

Shopping for local crafts in Rwanda is an immersive experience that connects you to the country's vibrant culture and skilled artisans. Whether you're picking up a handwoven basket or a beautiful piece of art, these markets and shops offer more than just souvenirs—they offer a deeper connection to Rwanda's traditions.

CHAPTER 10

Experiencing Rwanda: Food, Festivals, and Local Life

Rwanda offers a rich experience for the senses, from its flavorful dishes to vibrant festivals and skilled craftsmanship. Savor local meals, engage in lively cultural celebrations, explore traditional crafts, and connect with locals to understand the soul of Rwanda. Each experience deepens your connection to the country's true essence.

Must-Try Rwandan Dishes: A Culinary Adventure

Rwanda's food scene offers a beautiful blend of fresh, local ingredients and traditional flavors. From hearty stews to sweet, starchy dishes, Rwandan cuisine is not just about food but about experiencing the culture and history of the country. Here are five essential dishes that you shouldn't miss during your visit to Rwanda.

1. Isombe (Cassava Leaves with Peanut Sauce)
Main Ingredients:
The dish consists of cassava leaves, peanut paste, garlic, onion, and oil. Some versions may also include meat or fish for added flavor.

Preparation and Taste:
Isombe is prepared by cooking cassava leaves with a mixture of peanuts and spices until soft. The resulting dish is savory with a nutty, earthy flavor that pairs perfectly with starchier side dishes like ugali or plantains.

Price Range:
Between RWF 1,500 and RWF 3,000 ($1.50 - $3), depending on where you eat.

Where to Find It:

- Heaven Restaurant (Kigali) – GPS: 1.9570° S, 30.0968° E
- Kigali Serena Hotel (Kigali) – GPS: 1.9561° S, 30.0610° E
- The Hut Restaurant (Kigali) – GPS: 1.9570° S, 30.0648° E

Dining Tips:
Traditionally served with starches like rice or sweet potatoes, Isombe is often enjoyed as a communal meal. Try it with Icyayi, a local tea.

2. Ugali (Maize Porridge)
Main Ingredients:
Maize flour and water are the basic ingredients for Ugali, a staple food in Rwanda. It's often paired with stews and vegetables.

Preparation and Taste:
Ugali is made by cooking maize flour in water until it thickens into a dense, sticky porridge. It has a neutral taste and is used to complement richer stews or grilled meats.

Price Range:
RWF 500 to RWF 1,500 ($0.50 - $1.50)

Where to Find It:

- Café Kigali (Kigali) – GPS: 1.9474° S, 30.0610° E
- Chez Lando (Kigali) – GPS: 1.9512° S, 30.0586° E
- The Bistro (Kigali) – GPS: 1.9594° S, 30.1189° E

Dining Tips:
Ugali is usually eaten by tearing off small pieces and using it to scoop stews or vegetables. It's typically enjoyed at lunch or dinner.

3. Brochettes (Grilled Meat Skewers)
Main Ingredients:
Beef, goat, or chicken, marinated in spices, and grilled over an open flame.

Preparation and Taste:
Brochettes are skewers of marinated meat, often grilled and served with sides like fried plantains or salads. The meat is tender and smoky, with a rich and savory flavor from the marinade.

Price Range:
RWF 2,000 to RWF 5,000 ($2 - $5)

Where to Find It:
- Shokola Grill (Kigali) – GPS: 1.9449° S, 30.0601° E
- Bourbon Café (Kigali) – GPS: 1.9541° S, 30.0624° E
- The Kigali Cultural Village – GPS: 1.9566° S, 30.1060° E

Dining Tips:
Brochettes are perfect for a casual lunch or dinner. Pair them with a cold Rwandan beer like Primus or Mützig for an authentic experience.

4. Ibihaza (Pumpkin with Beans)
Main Ingredients:
Pumpkin, beans, onion, and spices like ginger and garlic.

Preparation and Taste:
Ibihaza is prepared by cooking pumpkin and beans together, creating a rich, sweet and savory dish. It's often served with rice or ugali. The flavors are earthy and comforting.

Price Range:
RWF 1,000 to RWF 2,500 ($1 - $2.50)

Where to Find It:
- Iris Café (Kigali) – GPS: 1.9508° S, 30.0874° E
- Inzora Rooftop Café (Kigali) – GPS: 1.9470° S, 30.0610° E
- Chez Nyira (Ruhengeri) – GPS: 1.4970° S, 29.7343° E

Dining Tips:
Often served as a main course for vegetarians, it can also be enjoyed with grilled meats for a more filling meal.

5. Agatogo (Vegetable Stew with Plantains)
Main Ingredients:
Plantains, beans, carrots, and tomatoes.

Preparation and Taste:
Agatogo is a hearty stew where plantains are boiled with vegetables, creating a creamy, savory dish. The plantains provide a smooth texture that pairs well with the tender beans and vegetables.

Price Range:
RWF 1,500 to RWF 3,000 ($1.50 - $3)

Where to Find It:
- Kigali Genocide Memorial Café – GPS: 1.9463° S, 30.0606° E
- Chez Nelly (Kigali) – GPS: 1.9511° S, 30.0601° E
- The Kabuye Market (Kibuye) – GPS: 1.9117° S, 29.3703° E

Dining Tips:
A staple in rural areas, Agatogo is often served at lunch or dinner with ugali or brochettes. It's typically eaten with family or as part of a community gathering.

Dining Etiquette and Useful Phrases

In Rwanda, meals are often shared in large groups, reflecting the importance of community. Bargaining is not common in restaurants, but if you're shopping at markets, don't hesitate to ask for a lower price. Some useful phrases include:

- "Muraho" (Hello)
- "Murakoze" (Thank you)
- "Ibyiza" (Delicious)

Rwandan cuisine offers a satisfying blend of hearty meals and vibrant flavors. Whether you're sampling a local stew or enjoying grilled meats, each dish is a testament to the country's rich culinary traditions. Don't miss the chance to experience Rwanda's flavors and culture firsthand.

Rwandan Festivals: Celebrate the Culture and Traditions

Rwanda is a country rich in history, culture, and vibrant traditions, all of which are showcased during its many festivals. These events are a wonderful opportunity for visitors to experience the heart of Rwanda and participate in unique celebrations that bring communities together. Whether it's music, dance, or cultural rituals, Rwanda's festivals are a window into the nation's soul.

1. Kwita Izina – The Gorilla Naming Ceremony

Date and Overview:

Kwita Izina, held in September, is Rwanda's premier festival, celebrating the birth of newborn gorillas in the Volcanoes National Park. This event, known as the Gorilla Naming Ceremony, allows attendees to witness the naming of young gorillas while raising awareness about conservation efforts.

Key Venues and Hotspots:
- Volcanoes National Park (Ruhengeri, Northern Rwanda)
- Kigali Convention Centre (Kigali)
- GPS: 1.9497° S, 30.0584° E

Opening Hours:

Typically lasts all day, with the ceremony held in the morning, followed by related cultural performances and environmental awareness campaigns throughout the day.

Dress Code:

Comfortable, light clothes are recommended, especially if you're visiting the park for gorilla trekking. For the ceremony, smart casual or traditional attire is appropriate.

Festival Etiquette:
- Respect local customs and ceremonies
- Don't approach the animals too closely during the trek or ceremony
- Be mindful of the environment and leave no trace behind

How to Get Around:

In Kigali, taxis, private transport, or shuttle buses provided by the festival organizers are common options. For access to Volcanoes

National Park, hiring a local guide is recommended for safety and better navigation.

Budgeting and Expenses:
Tickets for the ceremony and gorilla trekking can cost between $150 to $1,500. Budget for meals, accommodations, and transportation, which can add up to $500 - $1,000 depending on your choice of lodging and activities.

Local Laws and Regulations:
- Permits: A gorilla trekking permit is required. Permits should be secured months in advance.
- Conservation laws: Strict guidelines protect the gorillas and the park's environment. Respect the wildlife and local customs.

2. Umuganura – The Rwandan Harvest Festival
Date and Overview:
Held in August, Umuganura is Rwanda's harvest festival, a time for Rwandans to come together and celebrate the year's agricultural successes. This festival is deeply rooted in Rwanda's farming traditions.

Key Venues and Hotspots:
- Kigali (Citywide celebrations)
- Gisenyi (Near Lake Kivu for lakeside celebrations)
- GPS: 1.6917° S, 29.2400° E

Opening Hours:
Celebrations start early in the morning with local markets, cultural performances, and community meals.

Dress Code:

Traditional Rwandan attire is often worn for the festival, including Kitenge (colorful fabric). For visitors, comfortable, casual clothing is acceptable.

Festival Etiquette:
Participate in communal meals and share stories of harvest.
Be respectful during cultural dances and performances.

How to Get Around:
Local taxis, boda-bodas (motorcycle taxis), and organized tours can help you get around during the festival.

Budgeting and Expenses:
While the event itself is free, expect to spend on food, souvenirs, and transport. Budget approximately $20 - $50 for a day's experience.

Local Laws and Regulations:
Respect for nature: During Umuganura, it's customary to offer thanks to nature, so be mindful of waste and environmental practices.

3. KigaliUp Festival
Date and Overview:
This annual music festival celebrates Rwandan and international music artists. Held in July, it's one of East Africa's premier music festivals and showcases Rwanda's rich music scene alongside international performances.

Key Venues and Hotspots:
- Kigali Convention Centre (Kigali)
- Amahoro National Stadium (Kigali)
- GPS: 1.9614° S, 30.0994° E

Opening Hours:

The festival runs for several days, usually starting in the afternoon until late at night.

Dress Code:
Casual or concert attire, comfortable shoes for dancing, and light clothing due to the outdoor venue.

Festival Etiquette:
Respect personal space at concerts and festivals.
Be mindful of local customs when interacting with the performers and audience.

How to Get Around:
Public transport is available, but taxis and ride-hailing apps like SafeMotos are often faster and more convenient during large festivals.

Budgeting and Expenses:
Tickets for KigaliUp typically range from RWF 5,000 to RWF 20,000 ($5 - $20), depending on seating and stage access. Transportation and food are additional costs.

Local Laws and Regulations:
Alcohol consumption is regulated at festivals. Ensure you comply with local drinking laws.

4. Rwanda Film Festival (Hillywood)
Date and Overview:
Held in July, this is Rwanda's premier film festival showcasing local and African cinema. The event encourages cultural exchange and highlights Rwanda's growing film industry.

Key Venues and Hotspots:
- Kigali Serena Hotel
- Kigali City Tower
- GPS: 1.9561° S, 30.0609° E

Opening Hours:
Screenings take place in the evenings, with some daytime events for discussions.

Dress Code:
Smart casual for screenings and red carpet events.

Festival Etiquette:
Avoid using phones during screenings and be respectful of filmmakers and audiences.

How to Get Around:
Public transport or taxis are convenient, but be cautious at night.

Budgeting and Expenses:
Ticket prices typically range from RWF 1,000 - RWF 5,000 ($1 - $5) for screenings.

Local Laws and Regulations:
No photography during screenings without prior permission.
Respect for cultural values is key.

Rwanda's festivals are an immersive experience that allows visitors to connect deeply with the culture. Whether you're attending a music festival, a harvest celebration, or a film festival, each one provides a unique opportunity to celebrate the country's history, traditions, and vibrant community spirit.

Traditional Crafts: A Souvenir Shopper's Guide

Rwanda is home to a vibrant artisan culture, with traditional crafts that reflect the country's rich heritage. Whether you're seeking a memorable souvenir or looking to connect with the local culture, here are four traditional crafts you should definitely check out while visiting Rwanda.

1. Handwoven Baskets (Agaseke)

Description:
Rwandan baskets, known as Agaseke, are intricately woven by skilled artisans. Traditionally used for carrying food, they are now popular as decorative items. These baskets are typically made from grass, palm leaves, and banana fibers, with designs that symbolize various aspects of Rwandan life, including unity and peace.

Where to Find:
- Kimironko Market, Kigali – GPS: 1.9474° S, 30.1259° E
- Caplaki Craft Village, Kigali – GPS: 1.9571° S, 30.1066° E
- The Inema Arts Centre, Kigali – GPS: 1.9463° S, 30.0902° E

How to Get There:
Kimironko Market is a short drive from the city center. Caplaki Craft Village is easily accessible by taxi or private transport. Inema Arts Centre is located near the city center and is also reachable by taxi.

Other Things to Shop For:
You can also find wooden carvings, beaded jewelry, and handmade textiles in these markets.

Bargaining:
Bargaining is common, but always be respectful. Start by offering 30-40% less than the asking price and negotiate in good faith.

Opening Hours:
- Kimironko Market: Daily from 6:00 AM - 6:00 PM
- Caplaki Craft Village: 9:00 AM - 6:00 PM
- Inema Arts Centre: 9:00 AM - 5:00 PM

Payment Methods:
Cash (Rwandan Francs, USD), and some vendors accept mobile payments via M-Pesa or Airtel Money.

Haggling Etiquette:
Be polite and never overly aggressive when bargaining. It's common to haggle for a better price, but always be respectful and reasonable.

2. Imigongo Art (Cow Dung Paintings)
Description:
Imigongo is a traditional Rwandan art form created using cow dung mixed with natural pigments. The art features bold geometric patterns and vibrant colors, with symbolic meanings attached to each design. Imigongo paintings are typically used for decoration and storytelling.

Where to Find:
- Nyanza (Rwanda Art Museum) – GPS: 2.4344° S, 29.7382° E
- Kigali Art Museum – GPS: 1.9574° S, 30.0593° E
- Iby'iwacu Cultural Village, Nyundo – GPS: 1.6461° S, 29.8807° E

How to Get There:
Nyanza is about a 2-hour drive from Kigali, while Kigali Art Museum and Iby'iwacu Cultural Village are easily accessible within Kigali.

Other Things to Shop For:
Handcrafted wooden sculptures, traditional pottery, and woven mats are also available.

Bargaining:
While not as common in galleries, bargaining is accepted at cultural villages or markets. Be respectful when asking for a discount.

Opening Hours:
- Nyanza Museum: 9:00 AM - 5:00 PM
- Kigali Art Museum: 9:00 AM - 6:00 PM

Payment Methods:
Cash and mobile payments are commonly accepted.

3. Traditional Beadwork and Jewelry

Description:
Rwandan beadwork is crafted with glass beads and metal and is often used to make beautiful jewelry, such as necklaces, bracelets, and earrings. Each piece of jewelry often holds cultural significance and is made using intricate techniques passed down through generations.

Where to Find:
- Caplaki Craft Village, Kigali – GPS: 1.9571° S, 30.1066° E
- Kigali's Kimironko Market – GPS: 1.9474° S, 30.1259° E
- Rwanda Art Museum Shop – GPS: 1.9604° S, 30.1040° E

How to Get There:
Accessible by taxi, with Caplaki Craft Village and Kimironko Market located close to each other.

Other Things to Shop For:
Handwoven baskets, wood carvings, and textiles are also popular items to purchase.

Bargaining:
Bargaining is a common practice, especially at markets, where prices are typically marked higher than what the seller is willing to accept.

Opening Hours:
Caplaki Craft Village: 9:00 AM - 6:00 PM
Kimironko Market: 6:00 AM - 6:00 PM

Payment Methods:
Cash is widely accepted, as well as mobile money.

4. Traditional Pottery
Description:
Rwandan pottery is traditionally used for cooking and storing food. The pottery is made by hand, often using clay and other local materials. The pottery varies from simple everyday items to decorative pieces, reflecting the creativity of the artisan.

Where to Find:
- Gisenyi Market, Lake Kivu – GPS: 1.7000° S, 29.2500° E
- Kigali Craft Market – GPS: 1.9521° S, 30.0615° E
- Rwanda Cultural Village, Nyundo – GPS: 1.6461° S, 29.8807° E

How to Get There:
Gisenyi is located near Lake Kivu, about a 3-hour drive from Kigali. Kigali Craft Market is easily accessible within the city.

Other Things to Shop For:
Textiles, traditional tools, and basketry are other popular items.

Bargaining:
Bargaining is common, especially at markets. Always keep a friendly tone when negotiating.

Opening Hours:
Gisenyi Market: 6:00 AM - 6:00 PM
Kigali Craft Market: 9:00 AM - 5:00 PM

Payment Methods:
Cash (Rwandan Francs, USD), and mobile payments.

Safety, Etiquette, and Language Tips
Safety:
Always keep an eye on your belongings, especially in crowded markets. Stick to well-lit areas at night.

Etiquette:
When shopping, it's important to engage respectfully with the sellers. Be polite and patient when negotiating.

Useful Phrases:
- "Muraho" (Hello)
- "Murakoze" (Thank you)
- "Ndagura" (I want to buy)

How to Connect with Locals: Tips for Meaningful Interactions

Rwanda's people are known for their warmth, hospitality, and resilience. Connecting with locals can enrich your travel experience and offer a deeper understanding of the country's culture, values, and daily life. Here are some tips to ensure that your interactions are respectful, meaningful, and rewarding.

1. Learn Basic Kinyarwanda Phrases
Kinyarwanda is Rwanda's official language, and while many Rwandans speak English and French, making the effort to learn a few basic phrases can go a long way in building rapport with locals. Here are a few phrases to help you get started:

Muraho (Hello)
Murakoze (Thank you)
Amakuru (How are you?)
Nishimiye kukubona (Nice to meet you)
These small efforts will be appreciated and open doors to warmer interactions.

2. Respect Local Customs and Traditions
Rwandans are proud of their heritage, and learning about their customs will help you interact more meaningfully. For example, when visiting a home, it is common to greet elders first, and you may be offered food or drink as a sign of hospitality. Accepting these offerings with gratitude is a sign of respect. If invited to a meal, it's polite to eat with your right hand, as the left hand is considered impolite.

3. Participate in Community Activities

Many Rwandan communities encourage visitors to participate in local activities, such as community clean-up projects, dance performances, or farming activities. This is a great way to bond with locals and learn about their way of life. The Umuganda, a monthly community work day on the last Saturday of each month, is a national tradition where citizens come together to improve their neighborhoods. Participating in such activities can give you insight into Rwanda's strong sense of unity.

4. Be Patient and Open-Minded

Rwandans are known for their calm and measured approach to life. When engaging with locals, it's important to be patient and open-minded. While Rwanda has become a modern and thriving country, some regions are more rural, and daily life may unfold at a slower pace. Embrace the slower rhythm, and you will find your interactions more meaningful.

5. Share a Meal or Drink

Sharing a meal or a cup of tea with locals is one of the best ways to connect in Rwanda. Many Rwandans take pride in preparing Isombe (cassava leaves with peanut paste) or Brochettes (grilled meat skewers), and sharing such a dish over conversation is a wonderful experience. If you're in a rural village, being invited to a communal meal can also be a way to learn about the region's food culture and farming practices.

6. Ask Questions and Show Genuine Interest

Rwandans love to share their stories, especially about their country's recovery and transformation. If you approach conversations with respect and curiosity, most locals will be eager to engage with you. Ask about their experiences, the history of their communities, or their favorite local spots. Listening attentively is just as important as speaking.

7. Be Respectful of Privacy
While Rwandans are generally friendly and welcoming, they also value their privacy. Avoid overly personal questions unless the relationship is well-established, especially regarding topics like family life or past struggles. Showing respect for personal boundaries will foster more trust in your interactions.

8. Use Local Transport and Support Local Businesses
Engaging with local businesses, whether through small markets or local restaurants, is a fantastic way to interact and support the community. Taxis and motorbike taxis (boda-bodas) are commonly used for transport, and local shops often sell handmade goods such as jewelry, baskets, and textiles.

Connecting with locals in Rwanda isn't just about exchanging words; it's about embracing the culture, traditions, and stories that make the country special. By learning a bit of the language, respecting customs, and participating in local life, you'll find that the people of Rwanda will not only share their culture with you but will welcome you as part of their extended family. These connections will make your travel experience far more meaningful, and you'll return home with memories that last a lifetime.

CHAPTER 11

Itinerary Planner

Whether you're seeking adventure, cultural insights, or a family-friendly journey, Rwanda offers an array of experiences to suit every interest. From a 1-week adventure to an in-depth 10-day exploration, this section provides detailed itineraries to help you make the most of your time in Rwanda.

1-Week Adventure: A Comprehensive Tour of Rwanda

A week in Rwanda offers the perfect opportunity to experience the country's spectacular wildlife, rich history, and vibrant culture. Whether you are a nature enthusiast, a history buff, or simply in search of adventure, this comprehensive tour is designed to make the most of your time in Rwanda. Here's a detailed itinerary for an exciting and immersive one-week adventure.

Day 1: Arrival in Kigali

Arriving in Kigali, Rwanda's bustling capital, you'll quickly notice the blend of modernity and tradition. Spend your first day exploring the city's highlights. A visit to the Kigali Genocide Memorial is a poignant and important experience, providing insight into Rwanda's history and resilience.

What to Do:
Visit the Kigali Genocide Memorial and the Kimironko Market.
Enjoy a meal at Heaven Restaurant, known for its delicious local and international dishes.
Take a stroll around Kigali's craft markets for a taste of local art and crafts.

Estimated Budget:
- Accommodation: Budget hotels range from $50 - $100 per night.
- Food: $10 - $20 per meal at local restaurants.
- Transportation: Taxi or car hire will cost around $20 - $40 per day.

Day 2-3: Volcanoes National Park

On Day 2, journey to Volcanoes National Park, located about a 2.5-hour drive from Kigali. Home to the endangered mountain gorillas, this park offers the opportunity to go gorilla trekking, one of the most sought-after wildlife experiences in Africa. Trekking through the lush, misty forest is both challenging and rewarding, as you come face-to-face with the gentle giants.

What to Do:
Gorilla Trekking: Spend a day trekking through the park, where guides will help you locate the gorillas.
Visit Iby'iwacu Cultural Village for an interactive experience of Rwandan culture, traditional dances, and music.
Take a scenic drive around the park for magnificent views of the Virunga Mountains.

Estimated Budget:
- Gorilla Trekking Permit: $1,500 per person.
- Accommodation: Stay in mid-range lodges for around $100 - $150 per night.
- Meals: Around $20 - $30 per meal.
- Transportation: Private transfers to Volcanoes National Park can cost around $100 - $150 per day.

Day 4: Lake Kivu

After your adventure with the gorillas, take a drive to Lake Kivu for a peaceful retreat. This beautiful freshwater lake, surrounded by hills, offers a calm environment where you can unwind. Explore the lakeside town of Gisenyi, where you can enjoy boat rides, kayaking, or simply relax by the water.

What to Do:
Take a boat tour of Lake Kivu and visit nearby islands.
Enjoy a kayak ride or fishing excursion.
Relax on the beaches of Gisenyi or visit local villages.

Estimated Budget:
- Accommodation: Lakeside hotels range from $60 - $120 per night.
- Boat Tour: Around $20 - $40 per person.
- Meals: About $15 - $25 per meal.

Day 5-6: Nyungwe National Park

On Day 5, head south to Nyungwe National Park, a tropical rainforest known for its biodiversity and trekking opportunities. Nyungwe is one of the best places for chimpanzee trekking in Rwanda. The park also offers scenic hikes and the famous Canopy Walk that gives you a bird's-eye view of the forest below.

What to Do:
Chimpanzee Trekking: Spend a day tracking chimpanzees in the wild. Hike the Waterfall Trail or enjoy the Canopy Walk for stunning views. Visit the Nyungwe Forest Lodge for a luxurious retreat.

Estimated Budget:
- Chimpanzee Trekking Permit: $90 - $100 per person.
- Accommodation: Lodges range from $100 - $200 per night.
- Meals: About $20 - $30 per meal.

Day 7: Return to Kigali
On your last day, return to Kigali, where you can visit any spots you missed or shop for souvenirs at the local markets. End your trip with a relaxing dinner at one of Kigali's rooftop restaurants, offering stunning views of the city.

What to Do:
Kigali Arts and Crafts Market for souvenirs.
Visit the Rwanda Art Museum or relax in one of the city's cafes.

Estimated Budget:
- Accommodation: Budget hotels or guesthouses cost about $50 - $100 per night.
- Meals: $10 - $20 per meal.

Total Estimated Budget for 1-Week Adventure:
- Accommodation: $400 - $1,100
- Meals: $150 - $250
- Activities and Permits: $2,000 - $2,500 (including permits for gorilla and chimpanzee trekking)
- Transportation: $200 - $400 (including taxis, private transfers, and boat rides)

10-Day Expedition: Cultural and Wildlife Exploration

Rwanda is a country of extraordinary beauty, rich culture, and vibrant wildlife, offering a perfect blend of adventure, relaxation, and immersion into local life. This 10-day itinerary is designed for travelers who want to explore Rwanda's wildlife, culture, and history in depth. From its world-renowned gorilla trekking to its welcoming local communities, this journey will leave you with lasting memories and a deeper appreciation of this East African gem.

Day 1: Arrival in Kigali – Rwanda's Capital
Overview:
Arrive in Kigali, Rwanda's vibrant capital, known for its clean streets, bustling markets, and rich history. Start your exploration by visiting the Kigali Genocide Memorial, a poignant experience that offers insight into Rwanda's past and its path toward healing and unity.

Activities:
- Visit the Kigali Genocide Memorial.
- Explore Kimironko Market, where you can find local crafts and fresh produce.
- Have dinner at Heaven Restaurant, offering a mix of Rwandan and international cuisine.

Estimated Budget:
- Accommodation: $50 - $100 per night
- Meals: $15 - $25 per meal
- Transportation: $20 - $30 for a taxi

Day 2-3: Volcanoes National Park – Gorilla Trekking
Overview:

Spend two days at Volcanoes National Park, home to the endangered mountain gorillas. Trek through lush forests and come face-to-face with these majestic creatures, experiencing one of the most extraordinary wildlife encounters in the world.

Activities:
- Gorilla trekking (permit required, $1,500 per person).
- Visit the Iby'iwacu Cultural Village to learn about Rwandan traditions.
- Relax and enjoy the surrounding views of the Virunga Mountains.

Estimated Budget:
- Gorilla Trekking Permit: $1,500
- Accommodation: $100 - $150 per night
- Meals: $20 - $30 per meal
- Transportation: $100 - $150 per day (private transfer to Volcanoes National Park)

Day 4-5: Lake Kivu – Peaceful Lakeside Retreat
Overview:
Travel to Lake Kivu, a stunning freshwater lake surrounded by mountains. This peaceful retreat offers boat rides, kayaking, and the opportunity to enjoy the stunning lakeside scenery.

Activities:
- Take a boat tour of the lake and explore nearby islands.
- Visit Gisenyi for lakeside activities, or simply relax by the shore.
- Enjoy a meal at Paradise Malahide, known for its lakeside view.

Estimated Budget:
- Accommodation: $60 - $120 per night
- Meals: $15 - $25 per meal

- Boat Tour: $20 - $40 per person

Day 6-7: Nyungwe National Park – Rainforest and Wildlife
Overview:
Nyungwe is one of Africa's most pristine tropical rainforests, home to chimpanzees, diverse bird species, and several hiking trails. Spend two days exploring this lush forest, taking in the sights and sounds of its unique wildlife.

Activities:
Chimpanzee trekking ($90 - $100 per permit).
Walk the Canopy Trail, offering a bird's-eye view of the forest.
Visit the Nyungwe Forest Lodge for a relaxing stay amidst nature.

Estimated Budget:
- Chimpanzee Trekking Permit: $90
- Accommodation: $100 - $150 per night
- Meals: $20 - $30 per meal
- Transportation: $150 - $200 (private transfer to Nyungwe)

Day 8-9: Akagera National Park – Safari Adventure
Overview:
Head to Akagera National Park for a classic African safari. Located in eastern Rwanda, Akagera is home to the Big Five (lions, elephants, buffaloes, leopards, and rhinos). Enjoy game drives and boat trips on Lake Ihema to observe wildlife in their natural habitat.

Activities:
- Game drives to spot the Big Five.
- Take a boat trip on Lake Ihema for birdwatching and wildlife sightings.
- Spend the night at Akagera Game Lodge, offering stunning views of the park.

Estimated Budget:
- Game Drive: $50 - $150 per person
- Accommodation: $80 - $120 per night
- Meals: $20 - $30 per meal
- Transportation: $100 - $150 per day

Day 10: Return to Kigali and Departure
Overview:
On your final day, return to Kigali for any last-minute shopping and sightseeing. Visit the Rwanda Art Museum for a final taste of Rwandan culture and creativity before your departure.

Activities:
- Visit the Rwanda Art Museum or do some shopping at the Kigali Arts and Crafts Market.
- Enjoy a farewell dinner at a local restaurant before heading to the airport.

Estimated Budget:
- Meals: $15 - $25 per meal
- Shopping and Souvenirs: $20 - $50
- Transportation: $20 - $30 for a taxi
- Total Estimated Budget for 10-Day Expedition:
- Accommodation: $800 - $1,500
- Meals: $200 - $350

Activities and Permits: $2,400 - $3,000 (including gorilla trekking, chimpanzee trekking, safari, and boat tours)
Transportation: $600 - $900 (private transfers and game drives)

Nature and Wildlife Lovers: An Itinerary for the Adventurous Traveler

Rwanda is a haven for nature and wildlife enthusiasts, offering rich ecosystems, lush landscapes, and rare encounters with wildlife. With its breathtaking views, diverse wildlife, and national parks brimming with life, Rwanda is a must-see for adventurous travelers. This itinerary is designed to make the most of your time, providing an immersive experience of the country's natural beauty and wildlife treasures.

Day 1: Arrival in Kigali – The Gateway to Rwanda
Your adventure begins in Kigali, the capital of Rwanda, which offers a warm welcome to all travelers. On your first day, get familiar with the city's surroundings, visit the Kigali Genocide Memorial for a sobering yet uplifting reflection on the nation's history, and enjoy the vibrant atmosphere of the capital.

Activities:
- Visit the Kigali Genocide Memorial to understand Rwanda's powerful journey of recovery.
- Walk through Kimironko Market to experience local culture and purchase handmade crafts.
- Enjoy a traditional Rwandan dinner at Heaven Restaurant, offering views of Kigali's skyline.

Estimated Budget:
- Accommodation: $50 - $100 per night
- Meals: $15 - $25 per meal
- Transportation: $20 - $30 for taxis within Kigali

Day 2-3: Volcanoes National Park – Gorilla Trekking Adventure
Next, head to Volcanoes National Park, where you will spend two days exploring the famous gorilla trekking experience. The park is home to over half of the world's remaining mountain gorillas, and this unique experience offers the chance to observe these magnificent creatures in their natural habitat.

Activities:
- Gorilla Trekking: A once-in-a-lifetime experience, where you'll trek through dense forest to meet the gorillas.
- Visit Iby'iwacu Cultural Village for cultural immersion, exploring traditional Rwandan lifestyles through dance, music, and craft-making.
- Hike the Virunga Mountains for panoramic views of the region.

Estimated Budget:
- Gorilla Trekking Permit: $1,500 per person
- Accommodation: $100 - $150 per night (mid-range lodges)
- Meals: $20 - $30 per meal
- Transportation: $100 - $150 per day (private transfers to the park)

Day 4-5: Lake Kivu – A Peaceful Escape
After the intensity of gorilla trekking, take a break by visiting Lake Kivu. Known for its pristine beaches and calm waters, the lake offers the perfect setting for relaxation and outdoor adventures. Stay in Gisenyi or Kibuye, two picturesque towns located by the lake.
Activities:

- Take a boat tour on Lake Kivu, exploring its small islands and scenic views.
- Visit Gisenyi for its lakeside beaches, where you can swim or relax.
- Explore Kibuye's local markets for souvenirs and crafts.

Estimated Budget:
- Accommodation: $60 - $120 per night
- Meals: $15 - $25 per meal
- Boat Tour: $20 - $40 per person
- Transportation: $100 - $150 per day

Day 6-7: Nyungwe National Park – Chimpanzee Trekking and Rainforest Exploration

From Lake Kivu, travel south to Nyungwe National Park, one of the most biodiverse rainforests in Africa. Spend two days trekking through the forest and enjoying the natural beauty. The park is home to chimpanzees, monkeys, and a variety of bird species. The Canopy Walk provides unique views of the forest's biodiversity.

Activities:
- Chimpanzee Trekking: Spend the day tracking chimpanzees in the wild.
- Walk along the Canopy Walk, suspended high above the forest floor for incredible views.
- Visit Nyungwe Forest Lodge for a peaceful retreat among the trees.

Estimated Budget:
- Chimpanzee Trekking Permit: $90 per person
- Accommodation: $100 - $200 per night (mid-range to luxury lodges)
- Meals: $20 - $30 per meal

- Transportation: $150 - $200 per day

Day 8-9: Akagera National Park – Safari in Eastern Rwanda
Head to Akagera National Park, Rwanda's premier safari destination, for two days of wildlife encounters. Akagera is home to the Big Five: elephants, lions, buffaloes, rhinos, and leopards, making it the perfect place for a traditional African safari.

Activities:
- Go on game drives to spot the Big Five and other wildlife.
- Enjoy a boat trip on Lake Ihema, offering opportunities for birdwatching and more wildlife sightings.
- Spend the night at Akagera Game Lodge, which offers comfortable accommodation with views of the park.

Estimated Budget:
- Game Drive: $50 - $150 per person
- Accommodation: $80 - $150 per night
- Meals: $20 - $30 per meal
- Transportation: $100 - $150 per day (private guide)

Day 10: Return to Kigali – Last-Minute Shopping and Departure
Your final day will be spent in Kigali. Use this time to explore more of the capital or shop for souvenirs before heading to the airport for your departure.

Activities:
Visit the Kigali Arts and Crafts Market for handmade souvenirs.
Enjoy a farewell dinner at The Bistro, where you can try local delicacies and international dishes.

Estimated Budget:
- Meals: $15 - $25 per meal
- Souvenir Shopping: $20 - $50
- Transportation: $20 - $30 for taxi rides around Kigali

Total Estimated Budget for Nature and Wildlife Lovers Itinerary
- Accommodation: $900 - $1,800
- Meals: $250 - $400
- Activities and Permits: $3,000 - $3,500 (gorilla trekking, chimpanzee trekking, game drives)
- Transportation: $600 - $1,000 (private transfers, game drives, boat tours)

Family-Friendly Rwanda: A Tailored Travel Plan for All Ages

Rwanda, often known for its captivating landscapes and wildlife, is also a fantastic family-friendly destination. From thrilling wildlife encounters to cultural experiences that educate and entertain, Rwanda offers a safe, welcoming environment for families with children of all ages. This tailored itinerary combines outdoor adventure, relaxation, and a taste of local culture, ensuring that everyone in the family—from toddlers to grandparents—will have an unforgettable time.

Day 1: Arrival in Kigali – The Gateway to Rwanda
Overview:
Your family adventure begins in Kigali, Rwanda's capital, where you'll be welcomed by friendly locals and a clean, modern city. Kigali is easy to navigate, making it a great starting point for families. Spend your first day acclimating and soaking up the city's welcoming vibe.

Activities:
- Visit the Kigali Genocide Memorial: A visit to this sobering yet inspiring site offers a chance for parents to explain Rwanda's history to older children in an age-appropriate way.
- Explore Kimironko Market: Perfect for a sensory experience where families can browse for local crafts, fruits, and spices.
- Relax at Inema Arts Center, which hosts a variety of cultural events and art exhibitions that engage children's creativity.

Estimated Budget:
- Accommodation: $60 - $120 per night (family-friendly hotels)
- Meals: $15 - $30 per meal at local restaurants
- Transportation: $20 - $40 for taxis or private transport

Day 2-3: Volcanoes National Park – Gorilla Trekking
Overview:
After Kigali, head to Volcanoes National Park, where the family can embark on one of the most iconic experiences in Rwanda: gorilla trekking. While younger children may not be able to trek to see gorillas, there are still opportunities to experience the wildlife through cultural programs and visits to the park's visitor center.

Activities:
- Gorilla Trekking: While this is suitable for children over the age of 15, families can split up, with one group trekking while the others visit the nearby Iby'iwacu Cultural Village, where traditional Rwandan dances and songs are performed.
- Visit the Twin Lakes of Ruhondo and Burera: Explore these peaceful lakes by boat or on a family-friendly hike around their shores.

Estimated Budget:
- Gorilla Trekking Permit: $1,500 per person
- Accommodation: $100 - $150 per night (family lodges)
- Meals: $20 - $30 per meal
- Transportation: $100 - $150 per day

Day 4-5: Lake Kivu – Relaxation and Water Activities
Overview:
After your wildlife adventures, unwind by the peaceful Lake Kivu, one of Africa's most beautiful freshwater lakes. The town of Gisenyi offers various activities, from boat rides to visiting local markets. This is a great place for families to relax and enjoy time together in a tranquil setting.

Activities:
- Boat Tour of Lake Kivu: Explore the serene waters, spotting birds and local villages along the shore.
- Relax at the Beach: The lakeside beaches are perfect for swimming and picnicking with the family.
- Visit Gisenyi's local market for souvenirs and handmade crafts to take home.

Estimated Budget:
- Accommodation: $60 - $120 per night (family-friendly hotels)
- Meals: $15 - $25 per meal
- Boat Tour: $20 - $40 per person
- Transportation: $80 - $100 per day

Day 6-7: Nyungwe National Park – Chimpanzee Trekking and Nature Walks
Overview:
Next, head to Nyungwe National Park, one of the oldest rainforests in Africa. The park offers a range of family-friendly activities, including

chimpanzee trekking and the famous Canopy Walk. The park's biodiversity will fascinate both young children and adults alike.

Activities:
- Chimpanzee Trekking: Children 12 and older can join a trek to see chimpanzees in the wild.
- Canopy Walk: A walk suspended high above the forest floor offers a thrilling perspective of Nyungwe's lush biodiversity.
- Visit the Nyungwe Forest Lodge, which offers a family-friendly retreat, complete with nature trails and birdwatching opportunities.

Estimated Budget:
- Chimpanzee Trekking Permit: $90 per person
- Accommodation: $100 - $200 per night
- Meals: $20 - $30 per meal
- Transportation: $150 - $200 per day

Day 8-9: Akagera National Park – Safari Adventure
Overview:
Head to Akagera National Park in eastern Rwanda for a true safari experience. This park offers an excellent chance to see the Big Five, including lions, elephants, buffaloes, leopards, and rhinos. Game drives are a great way to engage young ones with wildlife and nature.

Activities:
- Game Drives: Explore the park's varied ecosystems on a family-friendly safari.
- Boat Tour on Lake Ihema: Ideal for birdwatching and spotting hippos and crocodiles.
- Visit the Akagera Game Lodge, a comfortable base for the family with great views of the park.

Estimated Budget:
- Game Drive: $50 - $100 per person
- Accommodation: $80 - $150 per night
- Meals: $20 - $30 per meal
- Transportation: $100 - $150 per day

Day 10: Return to Kigali and Departure
Overview:
On your last day, return to Kigali, where you can visit the Kigali Arts and Crafts Market for souvenirs and gifts to remember your trip. A final meal at one of Kigali's family-friendly restaurants will allow you to reflect on your Rwanda adventure.

Activities:
- Visit the Kigali Arts and Crafts Market for a range of handmade crafts.
- Enjoy a final Rwandan meal at The Bistro before heading to the airport.

Estimated Budget:
- Meals: $15 - $25 per meal
- Souvenirs: $20 - $50
- Transportation: $20 - $30 for a taxi to the airport

Total Estimated Budget for a Family-Friendly 10-Day Adventure
- Accommodation: $900 - $1,600
- Meals: $250 - $400
- Activities and Permits: $3,000 - $3,500 (including gorilla trekking, chimpanzee trekking, safari activities)
- Transportation: $600 - $1,000 (private transfers, game drives, boat tours)

CONCLUSION

As your time in Rwanda comes to an end, you'll leave with more than just souvenirs or photos; you'll carry home a sense of deep connection to the country's extraordinary landscapes, its resilient people, and its vibrant culture. Your adventure in Rwanda leaves a lasting imprint, from the thrilling encounters with wildlife in Volcanoes National Park to the peaceful moments by Lake Kivu, and the rich stories shared by the locals.

Reflecting on Your Rwandan Adventure: Key Takeaways

Rwanda's beauty is unforgettable. From its sweeping hills to the mist-covered forests and thriving wildlife, the country offers an experience that will stay with you long after your visit. But it's not just the landscapes; it's the warmth of the people, the power of their resilience, and the country's efforts in healing and rebuilding that make Rwanda truly exceptional. As you reflect on your journey, think about the profound lessons of strength, hope, and community that Rwanda teaches through its past and present.

The Lasting Impact of Rwanda's Beauty and Resilience

Rwanda's landscape captivates with its natural beauty, but it's the resilience of its people that leaves the strongest impression. The country's journey from a painful past to a hopeful future is inspiring, and it's reflected in the pride Rwandans take in their land, culture, and conservation efforts. Whether you were moved by a visit to the Genocide Memorial or inspired by the efforts to protect the mountain gorillas, Rwanda's spirit will stay with you as a constant reminder of the strength that comes from overcoming adversity.

Preserving Memories: Tips for Documenting Your Journey

Rwanda offers endless opportunities to capture moments that will remind you of your time there. Whether you're snapping photos of the gorillas in the mist or taking in the view of Lake Kivu, documenting your journey will allow you to reflect on your adventure for years to come. Keep a travel journal to jot down the sights, sounds, and people you encounter. Purchasing local art or crafts is also a meaningful way to preserve memories and bring a piece of Rwanda back home with you.

When to Return: The Best Time for Your Next Visit

Rwanda is a destination that welcomes visitors year-round. However, the dry season from June to September is ideal for wildlife viewing, particularly for gorilla trekking, when trails are easier to navigate. The rainy season from March to May offers lush landscapes and fewer crowds, perfect for those looking to explore off the beaten path. No matter when you decide to return, Rwanda will always offer new experiences, from cultural festivals to wildlife adventures, ensuring your next visit is just as memorable as your first.

Made in United States
North Haven, CT
14 March 2025